A PASSAGE TO INDIA

India in 1924 was under the rule of the British, with all the social and political problems that accompany colonialism. The British lived in their own communities and there was little social contact between the two peoples. Indians, for example, were never allowed to belong to, or even enter, British clubs.

Adela Quested, young and idealistic, and impatient with these social attitudes, is full of enthusiasm for India. She has just travelled out from England with Mrs Moore, who is the mother of Ronny Heaslop. He is the city magistrate in Chandrapore, and there is an expectation that Adela and Ronny will marry, but meanwhile Adela intends to explore and learn. She is eager to meet and talk to Indians, and to see the 'real India'.

So when Dr Aziz, the charming Indian friend of Mr Fielding, the college headmaster, invites them all on an excursion to the famous Marabar Caves, Adela is delighted. Here at last is an opportunity to find the 'real India'. But what is the 'real India'? And even if Adela found it, would she understand it?

OXFORD BOOKWORMS LIBRARY
Human Interest

A Passage to India

Stage 6 (2500 headwords)

Series Editor: Jennifer Bassett
Founder Editor: Tricia Hedge
Activities Editors: Jennifer Bassett and Christine Lindop

E. M. FORSTER

A Passage to India

Retold by
Clare West

OXFORD UNIVERSITY PRESS

OXFORD

UNIVERSITY PRESS

Great Clarendon Street, Oxford OX2 6DP

Oxford University Press is a department of the University of Oxford.
It furthers the University's objective of excellence in research, scholarship,
and education by publishing worldwide in

Oxford New York

Auckland Cape Town Dar es Salaam Hong Kong Karachi
Kuala Lumpur Madrid Melbourne Mexico City Nairobi
New Delhi Shanghai Taipei Toronto

With offices in

Argentina Austria Brazil Chile Czech Republic France Greece
Guatemala Hungary Italy Japan Poland Portugal Singapore
South Korea Switzerland Thailand Turkey Ukraine Vietnam

OXFORD and OXFORD ENGLISH are registered trade marks of
Oxford University Press in the UK and in certain other countries

ISBN: 978 0 19 479271 4

Printed in China

ACKNOWLEDGEMENTS
The publishers would like to thank the following for permission to reproduce images:
Cover image courtesy of MGM Clip+Still / British Film Institute
The images in this edition are taken from the Thorn EMI Films production of *A Passage to India*,
1984, directed by David Lean. All material © 1984 Metro-Goldwyn-Mayer Studios Inc, supplied by
British Film Institute, Kobal Collection, Ronald Grant Archive and Photofest New York.

For more information on the Oxford Bookworms Library,
visit www.oup.com/bookworms

CONTENTS

PEOPLE IN THIS STORY

THE ENGLISH

Ronny Heaslop, *the City Magistrate in Chandrapore*

Mrs Moore, *Ronny Heaslop's mother*

Stella and Ralph Moore, *Mrs Moore's children by her second marriage*

Adela Quested, *a young woman who may marry Ronny Heaslop*

Cyril Fielding, *the headmaster of Government College*

Mr (Harry) Turton, *the Collector (the highest British official) in Chandrapore*

Mrs Turton, *Mr Turton's wife*

Major Callendar, *the Chief Medical Officer*

Mrs Callendar, *Major Callendar's wife*

Mr McBryde, *the Chief of Police*

Mrs McBryde, *Mr McBryde's wife*

Miss (Nancy) Derek, *a young woman in Chandrapore*

Sir Gilbert Mellanby, *Lieutenant-Governor*

Lady Mellanby, *Sir Gilbert's wife*

THE INDIANS

Aziz, *a doctor*

Hamidullah, *a lawyer*

Hamidullah Begum, *Hamidullah's wife, also Aziz's aunt*

Mohammed Latif, *a poor relation of Hamidullah*

Mahmoud Ali, *a lawyer*

Syed Mohammed, *an engineer*

Haq, *a police inspector*

the Nawab Bahadur, *a rich landowner in Chandrapore*

Professor Godbole, *a Hindu teacher at Government College*

Das, *a magistrate, assistant to Ronny Heaslop*

Amritrao, *a well-known lawyer from Calcutta*

PART ONE

Mosque

Except for the Marabar Caves, which are some distance away, the city of Chandrapore is not at all extraordinary. Its bazaars run along the bank of the Ganges, hardly distinguishable from the rubbish left by that great river. Its streets are narrow, its temples are unimpressive, and everything in it looks as if it is made of mud. When the Ganges floods, which happens occasionally, houses fall and people are drowned, but the general shape of the town remains, like some low but permanently surviving form of life.

Inland, there is a large sports ground, and a hospital. The railway station is on a small hill, and beyond the railway the land drops away and then rises again steeply. On this second hill live the English community. Viewed from their neat bungalows, Chandrapore appears a totally different place – a city of gardens, a tropical forest washed by a wide river. Between the bungalows are straight, well-kept roads; a red-brick clubhouse and a shop are conveniently situated nearby. There is nothing especially ugly here, but only the view is beautiful; the English community shares nothing with the city except the arch of the sky above.

By day, the blue of the sky turns pale and becomes white in the heat; after the sun has gone down, orange melts upwards into softest purple. But at night it is blue again, and then the stars hang like lamps from an enormously high roof. There are no mountains around; the land lies flat, rises a little, then is flat again. Only in the south, where a group of fists and fingers stand out against the sky, is the endless space interrupted. These fists and fingers are the Marabar Hills, containing the extraordinary caves.

1

A visit to a mosque

Abandoning his bicycle, which fell before a servant could catch it, the young man jumped up on to the veranda.

'Hamidullah, Hamidullah, am I late?' he cried excitedly.

'Aziz, do not apologize,' said his host. 'You are always late.'

'Kindly answer my question. Am I late? Has Mahmoud Ali eaten all the food? Mr Mahmoud Ali, how are you?'

'Thank you, Dr Aziz, I am dying.'

'Dying before your dinner? Oh, poor Mahmoud Ali!'

'Hamidullah here is actually dead. He died just as you rode up on your bicycle,' replied Mahmoud Ali.

'Yes, that is so,' said Hamidullah. 'Imagine us both speaking to you from another and happier world.'

'Does there happen to be such a thing as a pipe in that happier world of yours?'

'Aziz, don't be amusing. We're having a very sad talk.'

As he smoked the pipe, the smell of tobacco filled the room. It was delicious. Aziz lay back, relaxed, listening to the others. Their talk did not seem particularly sad – they were discussing whether or not it is possible to be friends with an Englishman. Mahmoud Ali argued that it was not, Hamidullah disagreed, but the discussion never became heated. Delicious indeed to lie on the wide veranda, with the moon rising in front and the servants preparing dinner behind, and no trouble happening.

'Look at my own experience,' Mahmoud Ali was saying.

'I only say that it is possible in England,' replied Hamidullah, who had studied in that country long ago.

'It is impossible here. The red-nosed boy, Heaslop, insulted me in court again today. I do not blame him. He was told that he ought to insult me. Until lately, he was quite a nice boy, but the others have got hold of him.'

'Yes, they come out from England intending to be gentlemen, and are told that is not suitable behaviour. Why, I remember when Turton came out first. You will not believe me, but I have driven with Turton in his carriage – the great Turton! Oh yes, we were once quite friendly. He has shown me his stamp collection.'

'He would expect you to steal it now. But Red-nose will be much worse than Turton!'

'I don't think so. They all become exactly the same. I give any Englishman two years – Turton or Burton, it is only the difference of a letter. All are exactly alike. Don't you agree?'

'I do not,' replied Mahmoud Ali, joining in the bitter fun, and feeling both pain and amusement at every word. 'Personally I find great differences among our rulers. Red-nose whispers, Turton talks clearly, Mrs Turton takes bribes, Mrs Red-nose doesn't and can't, because so far there is no Mrs Red-nose.'

'Bribes?'

'Didn't you know that a Rajah gave her a sewing machine in solid gold so that a canal would be built in his state?'

'And was it?'

'No, that is where Mrs Turton is so clever. When we poor blacks take bribes, we do whatever we are bribed to do, and the law discovers us. The English take, and do nothing. I admire them.'

'We all admire them. Aziz, please pass me the pipe.'

A servant announced dinner, but they ignored him. Mahmoud Ali remembered some urgent business, and went off in his carriage. 'Come and see my wife then, Aziz,' said Hamidullah, and they spent twenty minutes behind the purdah.

Hamidullah's wife, Hamidullah Begum, was Aziz's aunt, and enjoyed talking to him about the family. This led her to ask him a question. 'Now when are you going to get married?'

Respectful but annoyed, he said, 'Once is enough, Aunt.'

'Yes, he has done his duty,' added Hamidullah. 'Don't worry him. He continues his family line, with three children.'

'Aunt, they live most comfortably with my wife's mother.'

'And he sends them the whole of his salary, and tells no one the reason why he has no money. What more do you want?'

But Hamidullah Begum said, with great politeness, 'What will happen to all our daughters if men refuse to marry?' And both men immediately saw the strength of her argument. Marriage, motherhood, power in the house – for what else is woman born, and how can the man who has denied her these things live with his guilt? Aziz said goodbye to his aunt, murmuring as he usually did in this situation, 'Perhaps . . . but later . . .'

Aziz and his host sat down to dinner with Hamidullah's distant cousin, Mohammed Latif. He was a gentle, happy, and dishonest old man, who had never done any work in his whole life. As long as one of his relations had a house, he was sure of a home. Here the position he occupied was neither that of a servant, nor that of an equal. Aziz entertained them both by speaking aloud some of the many beautiful love poems he knew by heart.

Just then a servant arrived at the house and handed Aziz a note from the Chief Medical Officer, Major Callendar.

'Old Callendar wants to see me,' Aziz said, after reading the note. 'He might have the politeness to say why.'

'A case of serious illness, I dare say.'

'I dare say nothing. He has discovered our dinner hour, and chooses to interrupt us every time, to show his power.'

'There may be a professional reason, and you cannot be sure there isn't one,' said Hamidullah thoughtfully.

'I suppose I shall have to go. Mohammed Latif, my bicycle, please.' And as soon as the poor relation brought him the bicycle, Aziz jumped on and raced away from his friend's house. When a tyre went flat, he left the bicycle at another friend's house and found a carriage to take him the rest of the way. But at the Chief Medical Officer's bungalow, he discovered that Major Callendar had driven away half an hour before, and had left no message.

While he was arguing with the servant about this, two English ladies came out of the house. Aziz lifted his hat in greeting. They glanced at the Indian and turned quickly away.

'Mrs Callendar, it *is* a carriage,' the first one cried.

'Is it ours? Oh, let's take it anyway!' screamed the second, and both jumped in. 'Club, club, driver! Why doesn't the fool go?'

'Go, I will pay you tomorrow,' said Aziz to the driver in Urdu, and as they went off he called politely, 'You are most welcome, ladies.' They did not reply.

So it was the usual thing, just as Mahmoud Ali said – his greeting ignored and his carriage taken. He turned his back on the Callendars' bungalow and decided to walk home. But this was a type of exercise he was not used to, and quite soon he went into the courtyard of a mosque to rest.

He had always liked this mosque. He sat on a low wall in the courtyard, and looked at the front of the mosque, which was in full moonlight. Some day, he thought, he would build a mosque, smaller than this but just as perfect, so that all who passed by should experience the happiness he felt now. And near it he would be buried . . . Just then one of the columns of the mosque seemed to move. Belief in ghosts ran in his blood, but he sat firm. The column became an Englishwoman, who stepped out into the moonlight. Suddenly he was furiously angry and shouted, 'Madam! Madam! Madam!'

'Oh!' the woman gasped.

'Madam, this is a mosque, you have no right here at all. You should have taken off your shoes. This is a holy place.'

'I *have* taken them off. I left them at the entrance.'

'Then I beg you to forgive me.' The woman moved away from him. He called after her, 'I am truly sorry for speaking.'

'If I remove my shoes, I am allowed to enter?'

'Of course, but so few ladies take the trouble, especially if they think no one is here to see.'

'That makes no difference. God is here.'

'Madam, may I know your name?'

'Mrs Moore.'

Coming closer, he saw that she was old – her voice had deceived him. He did not know whether he was glad or sorry.

'Mrs Moore, I shall tell my friends about you. That God is here – very fine indeed. Can I call a carriage for you? You ought not to walk alone at night. There are bad people about, and snakes may come across from the Marabar Hills.'

'But you walk about yourself.'

'Oh, I am used to it.'

'Used to snakes?' They both laughed.

'I'm a doctor. Snakes don't dare bite me.' They sat down side by side in the entrance, and put on their shoes. 'May I ask you a question? Why do you come to Chandrapore?'

'To visit my son. He is the City Magistrate here.'

'Oh no, excuse me, that is quite impossible. Our City Magistrate's name is Mr Heaslop. I know him well.'

'He's my son, all the same,' she said, smiling. 'I was married twice. My first husband died, and so did my second.'

'Then is the City Magistrate your whole family now?'

'No, I have two younger children, Ralph and Stella.'

'Mrs Moore, this is all extremely strange, because like you I also have two sons and a daughter. Their names are Ahmed, Karim, and Jamila. Three children are enough, I think.'

She nodded, and for a while they were both silent, thinking of their families. She sighed, and rose to go.

'Would you care to see the Minto Hospital one morning?' he asked. 'I have nothing else to offer at Chandrapore.'

'Thank you, I have seen it already.'

'I suppose Major Callendar took you,' he said rather bitterly.

'Yes, and Mrs Callendar.'

His voice changed. 'Ah! A very charming lady.'

'Possibly, when one knows her better.'

'What? What? You didn't like her?'

'She certainly intended to be kind, but no, I didn't.'

He burst out, 'She has just taken my carriage! And Major Callendar interrupts my dinner, night after night, and doesn't even leave me a message! But what does it matter? I can do nothing and he knows it. I am just an Indian, my time is of no value . . .'

She listened. He was excited by the knowledge that someone sympathized with his wrongs. She had proved her sympathy by criticizing an Englishwoman, and his heart warmed to her.

'You understand me,' he cried. 'You know what we feel. Oh, if only other people were more like you!'

Rather surprised, she replied, 'I don't think I understand people very well. I only know whether I like or dislike them.'

'Then you are truly one of us.'

They walked together to the clubhouse. 'I'm sorry I'm not a member,' she said, 'I would have liked to ask you in.'

'Indians are not allowed in, even as guests,' he said simply. He turned away, feeling happy. As he walked downhill beneath the lovely moon, and again saw the beautiful mosque, he felt he owned the land as much as anyone did.

2

The Bridge Party

The performance of the musical 'Cousin Kate' was halfway through by the time Mrs Moore re-entered the club. Curtains were drawn, to prevent native servants seeing the ladies acting, and consequently the heat in the large room was almost unbearable. Mrs Moore had no desire to rejoin the audience, so she went into another, smaller room. The first thing she heard there was, 'I want to see the *real* India,' and her familiar world came back to her in a rush. This was Adela Quested, the strange, cautious girl whom Ronny had asked her to bring from England, and Ronny was her son, also cautious, whom Miss Quested would probably, though not certainly, marry, and she herself was an elderly lady.

'I want to see it too, and I only wish we could,' Mrs Moore replied. 'I think the Turtons are arranging something for next Tuesday.'

'It'll end in an elephant ride, it always does,' said Adela. 'Look at this evening. Imagine,"Cousin Kate"! What could be more boring than that? But where have you been? Did you succeed in catching the moon on the Ganges?'

'I went to the mosque, but I didn't see the moon on the river,' said Mrs Moore, who was tired after her walk. 'We don't see the other side of the moon out here, do we?'

'We aren't even seeing the other side of the world, that's my complaint,' said Adela. Mrs Moore agreed; she too was disappointed at the dullness of their new life. They had made such an exciting voyage across the Mediterranean and through the sands of Egypt to the harbour of Bombay, to find only a group of bungalows at the end of it. But she did not take the disappointment as seriously as Miss Quested, because she was older, and had learnt that life never gives us what we want at the moment that we consider it should. Adventures do occur, but not punctually.

'Mrs Moore, Miss Quested, have a drink,' said a pleasant voice. This was the Collector, Mr Turton, the most important British official in Chandrapore. He spoke to them for a while about Ronny, whom he clearly approved of. It wasn't that the young man was particularly good at sports or learning the language, or that he had much idea of the law, but – apparently a large but – Ronny was dignified. Miss Quested heard this with anxiety, as she had not decided whether she liked dignified men. Mr Turton continued, 'The long and the short of it is that Heaslop's a sahib; he's the type we want, he's one of us.'

Meanwhile the performance ended, and the band played the national anthem. Conversation stopped, faces stiffened. It was the anthem of the army of occupation. It reminded all present that they were British and in exile; it gave them strength to resist the natives a little longer. Then they relaxed, and offered each other drinks.

The two women refused – they had had enough of drinks – and Miss Quested, who always said exactly what was in her mind, announced again that she wanted to see the real India.

Ronny, who had just joined the two women, found the request amusing, and called out to a passer-by, 'Fielding! How is one to see the real India?'

'Try seeing Indians,' the man answered, and disappeared.

'Who was that?' asked Adela.

'Fielding, the headmaster at Government College.'

'As if one could *avoid* seeing them,' sighed Mrs Lesley, one of the older British wives.

'*I've* avoided it,' said Miss Quested. 'Except for my servant, I've scarcely spoken to an Indian since landing in India.'

'Oh, lucky you.'

'But I want to see them!' She became the centre of an amused group of ladies. One said, 'Wanting to see Indians! How new that sounds!' Another, more serious, said, 'Let me explain. I was a nurse before my marriage, and met a large number of them, so I know. Your only hope is to keep a good distance from them.'

'Even from your patients?' asked Mrs Moore.

'The kindest thing one can do to a native is let him die,' said the Chief Medical Officer's wife, Mrs Callendar.

'What would you say if he went to heaven?' asked Mrs Moore, with a gentle but pained smile.

'He can go where he likes as long as he doesn't come near me. I have a horror of them,' replied Mrs Callendar.

Just then Mr Turton interrupted their conversation. 'Would you like a Bridge Party, Miss Quested? The expression is my own invention – the idea is to make a bridge between East and West.'

'I only want to meet those Indians whom you meet socially as your friends,' said Adela, a little coldly.

'Well, we don't meet them socially,' he said, laughing. 'I'm sure they have many good qualities, but we just don't meet them.'

'I don't think much of that young lady,' Mrs Turton said to her husband as they drove away. 'I hope she hasn't been brought here to marry nice little Heaslop, but it looks like it.'

'You may be right, my dear,' said Mr Turton, who never

spoke against an Englishwoman if he could avoid it. 'But she's new to India, and naturally makes mistakes. India improves people's judgement. It has even improved Fielding.'

Mrs Turton closed her eyes at this name and remarked, 'Mr Fielding isn't pukka, and he'd better marry Miss Quested, because she isn't pukka either.'

Their departure from the club broke up the evening. At Chandrapore the Turtons were little gods; soon, however, they would retire to some suburban house in England, and die unknown and unremembered.

'It's very nice of the great man,' Ronny said, delighted at the politeness shown to his guests. 'Do you know, he's never given a Bridge Party before? I wish I could have arranged something, but when you know the natives better, you'll realize it's easier for him than for me. They know they can't deceive *him*, but I'm still new here. No one can even begin to think of knowing this country until he's been in it for twenty years. Here's an example of one of the mistakes I've made. I once asked one of the native lawyers to have a cigarette with me. I found afterwards that he'd told the whole bazaar that he was a favourite of mine. Ever since then I've been as stern as I could with him in court. It's taught me a lesson.'

'Isn't the lesson that you should invite *all* the lawyers to have a smoke with you?' asked Adela.

'Perhaps, but time's limited. I prefer to smoke at the club among my own people, I'm afraid.'

'Why not ask the native lawyers to the club?' she said.

'Not allowed.' He spoke pleasantly and patiently. Going to the veranda, he called to his servant to bring the carriage round.

Mrs Moore felt more awake outside, and looked up at the

sky. In England the moon seemed dead and far away; here she had a sudden feeling of being closely connected to the heavenly bodies. When she caught sight of the mosque at the turn of the road, she cried, 'Oh yes – *that's* where I've been!'

'But, mother, you can't do that sort of thing. It's not done. There's the danger from snakes, for one thing.'

'Ah yes, that's what the young man there said.'

'This sounds wonderful,' said Miss Quested, who was extremely fond of Mrs Moore. 'You meet a young man in a mosque, and then never let me know! Was he nice?'

Mrs Moore paused, then said firmly, 'Very nice.'

'Who was he?' Ronny asked.

'A doctor. I don't know his name. Rather small, with a little moustache and quick eyes. He called out to me, about my shoes.'

'I know of no young doctor in Chandrapore.'

'He didn't come into the club. He said he wasn't allowed to.'

Suddenly the truth struck him, and he cried, 'Good Heavens! An Indian! Why ever didn't you tell me you'd been talking to a native?' He began to question her crossly. 'He called to you in the mosque, did he? How? Was he rude to you?'

'He did seem a little rude at first,' admitted his mother, 'but as soon as I answered, he changed, and became quite charming.'

'You shouldn't have answered him, mother.' He was worried. It did not matter what his mother thought – she was just a visitor to India. But Adela might spend her life in the country, and it would be annoying if she started with the wrong idea about the natives.

When they reached his bungalow, Miss Quested went to bed,

and Mrs Moore had a short interview with Ronny. He wanted to ask about the Indian doctor in the mosque, because it was his duty to report suspicious characters. But when she mentioned the Minto Hospital, he was relieved, and said the man's name must be Aziz, and there was nothing against him at all. 'So you and he had a talk,' he went on. 'Did he seem to accept us British?'

'Yes, I think so, except – he doesn't care for the Callendars.'

'Told you that, did he? Major Callendar will be interested.'

'My dear boy! That was a private conversation. You mustn't pass it on to Major Callendar.'

'Nothing's private in India. A remark like that is the educated native's latest trick, especially the younger men. They do it to show their manly independence.'

'You never used to judge people like this at home.'

'India isn't home,' he replied rather rudely, but he was aware of being on uncertain ground, and was not surprised when his mother insisted that he should not repeat Aziz's remark.

'All right, mother, I promise. But in return, please don't talk about Aziz to Adela.'

'Not talk about him? Why?'

'I can't explain everything, mother. She'll begin worrying whether we treat the natives properly – and all that sort of nonsense.'

'But that's exactly why she's here. She wants to know more about your life here. She felt she had to come and see for herself before she – and you – decided. She's very, very fair-minded.'

'I know,' he said, sighing. The touch of anxiety in his voice made her feel that he was still a little boy, so she promised to do as he wished, and they kissed good night. Despite what her son had said, she still felt sure she was right in her own judgement.

❧

The Bridge Party, which took place in the clubhouse garden two days later, was not a success. Mrs Moore and Miss Quested arrived early, but the Indian guests had arrived even earlier, and stood crowded together at the far end of the garden.

'To work, Mary, to work,' cried the Collector to his wife.

Mrs Turton got up awkwardly from her seat. 'What do you want me to do? Oh, those purdah women! I never thought any would come. Oh dear!'

Some Indian ladies were standing in a separate little group, looking like colourful tropical birds, while their male relatives remained at a slight distance.

'I consider they ought to come over to me.'

'Come along, Mary, get it over with.' Her husband glanced down the line of Indian men. 'Whom have we here? H'm! Much as I expected. This one wants to do some work for us, and that one wants to ignore the building rules. They all have their own reasons for coming. Oh look! That carriage has smashed right into our flowers. Can't control his horse. They're all the same.'

'We ought not to have allowed them to drive into the club – it's so bad for them,' said Mrs Turton, who had at last begun her progress towards the Indian ladies, followed by Mrs Moore and Miss Quested. 'Why they come at all, I don't know. They hate it as much as we do.'

'Do kindly tell us who these ladies are,' said Mrs Moore.

'You're superior to them anyway. Don't forget that. You're superior to everyone in India except one or two of the princesses and you're equal to them.' She shook hands with the group and said a few words of welcome in Urdu. She only used the language to speak to her servants, so she knew none of the politer forms. Then she asked her companions, 'Is that what you wanted?'

'Please tell these ladies that I wish we could speak their language,' said Mrs Moore.

'Perhaps we speak yours a little,' one of the ladies said.

'Good Heavens, she understands!' cried Mrs Turton.

'But now we can talk. How delightful!' said Adela, her face lighting up. She now had her desired opportunity; friendly Indians were before her. She tried to make them talk, but failed

Adela tried to make the Indian ladies talk, but failed completely.

completely. Whatever she said, they agreed politely, smiling modestly and making uncertain little movements with their hands. Mrs Moore was equally unsuccessful. Mrs Turton watched, expressionless; she had known what nonsense it was from the beginning.

As she was saying goodbye, Mrs Moore suddenly said to one of the ladies, Mrs Bhattacharya, 'I wonder whether you would allow us to call on you some day – whenever is convenient.'

'All days are convenient,' she replied, charmingly.

'Thursday . . .'

'Most certainly.'

'It would be a real pleasure. What about the time?'

'All hours.' Mrs Bhattacharya gave the impression that she had known, since Thursdays began, that English ladies would come to see her on one of them, and so always stayed in. She added, 'We leave for Calcutta today.'

'Oh, but if you do,' cried Adela, 'then we shall miss you.'

Mr Bhattacharya called from the distance, 'Yes, yes, you come to us Thursday.' He added something to his wife in their own language.

'You haven't put off going just for us?' cried Mrs Moore. 'Oh, that would make me very unhappy!'

Everyone was laughing now, and a shapeless discussion took place, during which Mrs Turton left the group, smiling to herself. It was agreed that they would come on Thursday morning, and the Bhattacharya family would go to Calcutta later that day.

Meanwhile, the English had started playing tennis, and the Indian men were talking among themselves. The distance between East and West was increasing. The person who made the greatest effort to bring people together was Mr Fielding.

Cheerful and enthusiastic, he rushed from one group to another, making social mistakes which the parents of his pupils were happy to ignore, because he was popular among them. During his conversations, he heard what a success the two new ladies from England had been, and how their politeness in wishing to visit Mrs Bhattacharya had pleased not only her but all the Indians present.

He found the younger lady alone, looking over the garden at the distant Marabar Hills. And when he told her what pleasure she had given by her friendliness today, she thanked him so warmly that he asked her and the other lady to tea.

'We would love to come,' she replied. 'This party makes me so angry. Most of the English people here are being so rude to our guests. It makes me perfectly ashamed of them!'

Fielding hated the rudeness too, but he did not comment on it. Instead he asked if she was interested in Indian music, because there was a professor at the College who sang.

'Oh, just what we wanted to hear. And do you know Dr Aziz? Mrs Moore says he is so nice.'

'I know *of* him. I can ask him too, if you like. Shall we say Thursday afternoon?'

Adela accepted gratefully, and looked out at the hills. How lovely they suddenly were! But she couldn't touch them. In front of her, like a door closing, fell a vision of her married life. She and Ronny would visit the club every evening, then drive home to dress for dinner. They would see the Callendars and the Turtons and the Burtons, while the true India passed by unnoticed.

And sure enough they did drive away from the club in a few minutes, and they did dress for dinner. And they ate soup made from bottled vegetables, fish full of bones, more bottled vegetables with their meat, a sweet dish, and sardines on toast – the menu of British India. Dishes might be added or removed, but the tradition remained – the food of exiles, cooked by servants who did not understand it. Adela thought of the young men and women who had come to India before her, ship full after ship full, and had been given the same food and the same ideas, and been snubbed in the same good-humoured way until they began to snub others. She thought, 'I would never become like that.' But she knew this was something that was hard to resist, and she needed help. She must gather around her at Chandrapore a few people who felt as she did.

After dinner, when she had gone to bed, there was another interview between mother and son.

'Adela isn't worried about anything, is she?' Ronny began.

'Ask her, ask her yourself, my dear boy.'

'Probably she's heard stories of the heat, but of course every April I'd send her off to the hills, where it's cooler.'

'Oh, it wouldn't be the weather. It's much more the British themselves who are likely to worry Adela. She doesn't think they behave pleasantly to Indians, you see.'

'Oh, I knew it!' he cried, losing his gentle manner. 'How like a woman to worry over something so unimportant!'

'Unimportant? How can it be that?' she cried, surprised.

'We're not in India for the purpose of behaving pleasantly! We're here to do justice and keep the peace.'

'Your ideas are those of a god,' she said quietly.

Trying to recover his calm, he replied, 'India likes gods.'

'And Englishmen like pretending to be gods.'

'Look here, mother, what do you and Adela want me to do? Go against all the people I respect and admire here? Lose any power I have for doing good? I'm out here to work, remember, to hold this miserable country by force. We don't intend to be pleasant in India. We've something more important to do.'

He spoke sincerely. Every day he worked hard in the court, trying to decide which of two untrue accounts was the less untrue, trying to hand out justice fearlessly. He did not expect the Indians to be grateful – it was his duty – but he did expect sympathy from his own people.

His mother was not prepared to give him any. 'I think the English *are* out here to be pleasant,' she insisted. 'Because India is part of the earth. And God has put us on the earth to love our neighbours and to show it. And He is watching, even in India, to see how we are succeeding.'

He looked a little anxious. When she talked of religion, it reminded him that she was elderly and that he should not be angry with her. He said gently, 'I quite see that, mother. I suppose I should do a little work now, and you'll be going to bed.' Their conversation ended there. Mrs Moore felt she had made a mistake in mentioning God, but she found Him increasingly difficult to avoid as she grew older. God had been constantly in her thoughts since she entered India, but strangely enough He satisfied her less than ever before. Beyond the arch of the sky, there seemed always another arch, and beyond the most distant echo, a silence.

3
Tea with Mr Fielding

Mr Fielding was a good-tempered, intelligent man with a strong belief in education. He was a success with his pupils, but not with the English community. The men put up with him for his skill at sports and his cheerfulness; it was their wives who decided he was not really a sahib. He had discovered that it was possible to be friendly with Indians *and* Englishmen, but anyone wanting to be accepted by Englishwomen must drop the Indians. He preferred to spend time with Indians, so he seldom socialized with the English.

He lived in an eighteenth-century building close to the College. He was dressing after a bath, when Aziz arrived. 'Please make yourself at home,' he shouted from the bedroom.

Aziz was delighted. 'May I really, Mr Fielding? It's very good of you.' He glanced round the living room. 'I have long wanted to meet you. I have heard so much good about you.'

'And I know you very well by name. Oh no!'

'Anything wrong?'

'I've stood on my last collar-stud.'

'Take mine, take mine.'

'Not if you're wearing it yourself.'

'No, no, one in my pocket.' Unseen by Fielding, he pulled off his own collar and took out the back stud, a gold one that a relative had brought back from Europe for him. 'Here it is,' he cried.

'Come into the bedroom with it, if you don't mind.'

Replacing his collar, Aziz prayed it would stay in place

during tea. He entered the bedroom, and shook hands with his host. Fielding was not surprised at the speed of their friendship; with such an emotional people, it was likely to come at once or never.

While Aziz was fixing the stud into the back of Fielding's stiff collar, the Englishman said, 'Two ladies are coming to tea, Mrs Moore and Miss Quested.'

'Oh yes – I remember – an extremely elderly lady. I met her at the mosque. And another English lady? Just as you wish.' Aziz was disappointed that other guests were coming, as he wanted to be alone with his new friend.

'And Professor Godbole is coming too.'

'Ah yes, I know him. He is a Hindu, of course.'

How fortunate that it was an informal party! Aziz found the English ladies easy to talk to – he treated them like men. Beauty would have worried him, but Mrs Moore was so old and Miss Quested so plain that Aziz was spared this anxiety.

'I want to ask you something, Dr Aziz,' Adela began, as they sat down to tea under the shade of a tree in the garden. 'Can you explain a little disappointment we had this morning? I think we must have offended someone by mistake.'

'That is impossible, I'm sure. But may I know the facts?'

'An Indian lady and gentleman were to send their carriage for us this morning at nine. We waited and waited, but it never came.'

'May I know their name? Bhattacharya? Hindus, I think. They have no idea of society. It is as well you did not go to their house – it would give you a wrong idea of India. For myself, I think they grew ashamed of their house and that is why they did not send their carriage for you.'

'That's an idea,' said Fielding.

'I do so hate mysteries,' Adela announced.

'I like mysteries but I dislike confusion,' said Mrs Moore.

'Aziz and I know that India's all confusion,' said Fielding.

'There'll be no confusion when you come and see me,' said Aziz, a little uncertain about the way the conversation was going. 'Mrs Moore and everyone – I invite you all – oh, please do come.'

The old lady was glad to accept; she still thought the young doctor extremely nice. Adela accepted out of adventure, believing that when she knew him better, he would unlock his country for her. She asked him for his address.

Aziz thought of his bungalow with horror. It was a miserable little house in the bazaars, with practically only one room, which was always full of small black flies. 'Oh, but we will talk of something else now,' he said. 'Look at this beautiful house. I wish I lived here.'

The house had originally been built for some high official, and it was indeed beautiful. It was shaded by the surrounding trees in the garden, and the high-ceilinged rooms were cool and airy.

'Imagine I am a judge living in this house, as in the old days,' Aziz went on. 'I am doing justice. A poor widow who has been robbed comes to me and I give her fifty rupees, to another a hundred and so on. I would like that.'

'Rupees don't last for ever, I'm afraid,' Mrs Moore said.

'Mine would. God would give me more when he saw that I gave. We should always give, like the most generous man in Chandrapore, the Nawab Bahadur. And we would never punish anyone. Poor criminal, give him another chance.'

Aziz was unable to see that if the poor criminal goes free, he will again rob the poor widow. As he spoke, he felt affection for

'Look at this beautiful house,' said Aziz. 'I wish I lived here.'

everyone, even the English; he knew at the bottom of his heart that they could not help being so cold and strange and flowing like a stream through his land. He talked excitedly about his profession and his country. Mrs Moore smiled gently at him, her thoughts far away. But Adela in her ignorance thought he was 'India', and never realized his views were limited and his statements inaccurate.

Professor Godbole's arrival quietened him somewhat, but it remained Aziz's afternoon. In the middle of describing to Adela the joys of eating ripe mangoes, he said, 'Miss Quested, do stay for the mango season. Why not make your home in India?'

'I'm afraid I can't do that,' said Adela, without thinking what she was saying. Not for several minutes did she realize that it was an important remark and should have been made to Ronny first.

'Visitors like you are too rare.'

'They are indeed,' said the professor. 'But what can we offer to keep them here?'

'Mangoes, mangoes,' replied Aziz.

They all laughed. 'You can get mangoes in England now,' said Fielding. 'They take them by ship, in ice-cold rooms.' He turned to the old lady, who looked a little upset – he could not imagine why – and asked about her plans. She said she would like to see the College, and he offered to show her round. Adela said she would stay, so Fielding and Mrs Moore left the room.

The professor offered to send some special home-made sweets for Adela to try. 'Miss Quested, they are delicious,' Aziz said sadly. 'They will give you a real Indian experience. Ah, in my poor position I can give you nothing.'

'I don't know why you say that, when you have so kindly asked us to your house.'

He thought again of his bungalow with horror. Good Heavens, the stupid girl had taken him at his word! What was he to do? 'Yes, all that is arranged,' he cried. 'I invite you all to see me in the Marabar Caves.'

'I shall be delighted. What are they?'

'You have not heard of them?' Aziz and the professor cried together. 'The Marabar Caves in the Marabar Hills?'

'We hear nothing interesting up at the club. Only tennis and silly talk. Tell me everything about them, please.'

But when Aziz started to explain, it soon became clear that he had never visited the caves himself. He had always meant to go, but work or private business had prevented him, and they were so far away. Professor Godbole laughed at him pleasantly for this, but even the professor seemed unwilling or unable to say exactly what was so extraordinary about the caves.

Into this discussion came Ronny, calling across the garden with an annoyance he took no trouble to hide, 'What's happened to Fielding? Where's my mother?'

'Good evening!' Adela replied coolly.

'I want you and mother at once. There's going to be polo. I left work early because I thought you'd like to watch it.'

'Your mother will return shortly, sir,' said the professor, who had got up respectfully. 'There is little to see at our poor College.'

Ronny took no notice, but continued to speak to Adela. He did not mean to be rude to the two Indians – he simply forgot they were there. Unfortunately Aziz was in no mood to be forgotten. He did not get up, but called in an offensively friendly way, 'Come and join us, Heaslop, until your mother arrives.' Ronny replied by ordering one of the servants to fetch Fielding at once. Pretending to be helpful, Aziz corrected Ronny's Urdu and repeated the order. Ronny stood waiting in angry silence, and when his mother finally appeared, drew Fielding to one side.

'I say, old chap, do excuse me, but I think perhaps you shouldn't have left Miss Quested alone like that.'

'I'm sorry, what's the problem?' asked Fielding politely.

'I don't like to see an English girl left with two Indians.'

'She stayed with them by her own wish, you know.'

'Yes, that's all right in England, but out here . . . Can't you see that man's unreliable?'

Aziz, trying to recover the magic of the afternoon, was waving his arms about as he explained something to Mrs Moore. His manner was excitable, over-confident.

'He's fine,' protested Fielding. 'But I'm sorry if – well, never mind, it's over now. Take your ladies away with you.'

'Come to the polo with us, Fielding – we'd be delighted.'

But Fielding refused, and there were general goodbyes, with everyone feeling either cross or miserable. Suddenly Professor Godbole said, 'I may sing now,' and he did. His thin voice rose, giving out one sound after another, like the song of an unknown bird. Only the servants seemed to understand it, and they listened to it in delight, until, quite unexpectedly, it stopped.

'Thanks so much. What was that?' asked Fielding.

'It was a religious song. I say to Shri Krishna, "Come! Come to me only." The god refuses to come.'

'But he comes in some other song, I hope?' said Mrs Moore.

'Oh no, he refuses to come,' repeated Godbole, perhaps not understanding her question. 'I say to him, Come, come, come, come . . . But he does not come.' There was a moment of deep silence, not a leaf moving on the trees.

Although Adela had known Ronny well in England, she now felt relieved she had decided to see him here before agreeing to be his wife. India had developed sides of his character which she had never admired. How unpleasant he had been at Mr Fielding's! She wanted an opportunity to express her annoyance with him, and since he felt cross too, an opportunity soon presented itself.

In the carriage, she had only just started telling Mrs Moore about Dr Aziz's invitation to the Marabar Caves, when Ronny threw back his head and laughed.

'Have I said anything funny?' asked Adela coldly.

'I was only thinking how the good doctor's collar climbed up his neck. He was beautifully dressed, but he had forgotten his back collar-stud, and there you have the Indian all over – no attention to detail. Similarly, this idea of the Marabar Caves!'

'Have you been to them?' asked Adela.

'No, but I know all about them, naturally.'

'Oh, naturally!'

'Have *you* promised to go on this expedition, mother?'

'Mother has promised nothing,' said Mrs Moore surprisingly sharply. 'Certainly not to watch polo. Will you take me to the bungalow please? I prefer to rest.'

'Take me too,' said Adela. 'I'm not watching polo either.'

'Simpler to forget about polo altogether,' said Ronny. Tired and disappointed, he lost his self-control and added loudly, 'I won't allow you to be let down by Indians any more – if you want to go to the Marabar Caves, you'll be taken by the British.'

'I've never heard of these caves, I don't know where they are,' said Mrs Moore, 'but I really can't have' – she tapped the cushion beside her – 'so much quarrelling and unpleasantness!'

The young people were ashamed. They left her at the bungalow and drove together to the polo, feeling it was the least they could do. Adela was thinking over her own behaviour and didn't like it at all. Instead of giving careful consideration to her possible marriage and discussing her conclusions privately with Ronny, she had made a casual remark to a stranger, during a conversation about mangoes, that she didn't intend to stay in India. This meant that she wouldn't marry Ronny, but what a way to announce it, what a way for a civilized girl to behave!

The polo took place on the sports ground, and Ronny and Adela sat down on a seat some distance from the game. Adela took a deep breath and said, 'I've finally decided we are not going to be married, my dear boy.'

Ronny was very hurt, but he replied gently, 'You never said we would marry, my dear girl. Don't let this upset you.'

'I really can't have so much quarrelling and unpleasantness!'
said Mrs Moore.

How kind and reasonable he was! 'I'm so sorry to have given you and your mother all this trouble,' Adela said guiltily. 'Is there anything – you want to discuss?'

He was too proud to try to tempt her back. 'No, nothing. You've done quite right. It's no use talking further about it.'

'No use,' she repeated, feeling that one or both of them should have made a deeply passionate speech. 'We've been awfully British over it, but I suppose that's all right.'

'As we *are* British, I suppose it is,' he replied sadly.

'Anyway, we haven't quarrelled. I think we'll stay friends.'

'I know we shall.'

They both felt a wave of relief wash over them, and then

affection. Of course they were friends, and for ever. Adela moved a little closer to Ronny on the seat.

Just then the Nawab Bahadur, Chandrapore's richest and most hospitable landowner, appeared. He had been watching the polo, and offered them a drive in his new motor car. Thinking it might please Adela, Ronny accepted, and they got into the back of the car together, while the Nawab sat in front with his driver.

As the car rushed along the road, between the fields, darkness hid Ronny's face, an event which always increased Adela's respect for his character. Somehow her hand touched his, and neither withdrew it. Something in the air seemed to say that all their difficulties were only a lovers' quarrel.

Suddenly there was a bump and the car stopped. It was an accident. Adela had seen what had happened – the car had hit an animal of some kind and then run into a tree. Ronny permitted himself a moment's pause, then took control of the situation. No one was hurt but the car was damaged. Fortunately he was able to stop an English car which was passing, and he, Adela, and the Nawab returned to Chandrapore in it. Meanwhile the driver remained to guard the car and wait for a mechanic to repair it.

The excitement of the accident had brought Ronny and Adela closer together. They looked at each other when they reached Ronny's bungalow, and Miss Quested said nervously, 'Ronny, I would like to take back what I said on the sports ground.' He nodded, and as a result they were engaged to be married.

'Come along and let's tell mother about it,' he said, as they entered the house. And when the announcement was over, he made a generous offer. 'Look here, both of you, see India if you like and as you like – I know I made rather a fool of myself at Fielding's, but it's different now. I wasn't quite sure of myself.'

'My duties here are evidently finished,' thought Mrs Moore. 'I don't want to see India any more. I must go home and help my other children, if they need me.' She was tired by her visit to Government College and had been worried by the young people's argument. But she offered to play cards with Adela for the rest of the evening while Ronny worked on his papers. Outside, a strong wind blew up and passed away, leaving no freshness behind it; the hot weather was approaching.

4
Aziz and his friends

Aziz lay in bed in his bungalow, pretending to be very ill. He had a slight fever, which he would have ignored if there was anything important at the hospital. Now and then he groaned, and thought he was dying, but he did not think so for very long. It was Sunday, and the bells were ringing out from the English church – he did not object to them. He slept a little, and woke, and slept again. Sometimes he thought of women, the beautiful loose women he could meet in the Calcutta bazaars. Perhaps he could find an excuse to visit Calcutta, and persuade Major Callendar to give him a couple of days off. There was a man he knew in Calcutta who could send him a letter which he could show to the Major . . .

Suddenly he heard the noise of wheels outside his house. Someone had called to enquire about his health. The thought of sympathy increased his fever, and with a sincere groan he wrapped himself in his blanket. Three people came in and sat on his bed.

'Aziz, my friend, we are greatly concerned,' said Hamidullah.

'When a doctor falls ill, it is a serious matter,' said Mr Syed Mohammed, an engineer, bowing to Aziz.

'When an engineer falls ill, it is equally important,' said Mr Haq, a police inspector, bowing to Syed Mohammed.

'Oh yes, we are all very important, our salaries prove it!' said Hamidullah with a slightly bitter laugh.

They talked of health and Hindus, religion and politics. Aziz felt refreshed by the presence of his visitors, and his heart filled with emotion. Suddenly he threw off his blanket and began to speak the words of a long and beautiful poem in Urdu. The dirty little room grew quiet; even the black flies seemed to stop circling for a moment. Anxiety and annoyance fell away, and his guests listened with pleasure.

As he came to the end, he realized that another visitor had entered. It was Mr Fielding. All rose to their feet, except Aziz, who only said, 'Sit down,' rather coldly. What a room! What a meeting! He was embarrassed that Fielding would now see the poor conditions in which he lived.

'Well, are you ill or aren't you?' asked Fielding. He sat down on the side of the bed, refusing with a friendly smile the offer of a chair.

'No doubt the Major told you I'm pretending to be ill.'

'Well, *are* you pretending?'

The Indians laughed. 'An Englishman at his best!' they thought. 'So good-humoured!'

'He is ill and he is not ill,' said Hamidullah, offering a cigarette. 'And I suppose that is the same for most of us.'

Fielding agreed. He and the pleasant, sensitive lawyer were beginning to trust each other and become friends.

'The whole world seems to be dying,' continued Hamidullah, 'but it doesn't die, so we must assume that God exists.'

'I don't believe in God,' said Fielding.

A tiny movement of 'I told you so' passed round the group. 'Is that true for most people in England now?' Hamidullah asked.

'For educated, thoughtful people, yes. The truth is that the West doesn't worry much about belief or disbelief these days.'

'And does not morality also decrease?'

'It depends what you call – yes, yes, I suppose it does.'

'Excuse the question, but if so, how is England justified in holding India?' Hamidullah wanted to know.

'It's a question I can't really answer. It's beyond me. I'm out here because I need a job, that's all.'

'Well-qualified Indians also need jobs. Excuse me again – is it fair that an Englishman should occupy one, if an Indian is available? Of course I mean nothing personally. We are delighted you are here, and we benefit greatly from this honest talk.'

There is only one answer to a conversation of this kind: 'England holds India for the good of India.' But Fielding was too truthful to give it. 'I'm delighted to be here too,' he replied, 'and that's my only justification for being here.'

The Indians laughed. 'An Englishman at his best!'
they thought. 'So good-humoured.'

Soon afterwards the party broke up. They said goodbye to Aziz and went out on to the veranda. While they were waiting in the heat for servants to bring their horses out of the shade, Hamidullah said kindly to Fielding, 'Aziz has a high opinion of you. He only did not speak because of his illness.'

'I quite understand,' said Fielding, who was feeling rather disappointed with his visit. He had liked Aziz so much at their first meeting, and had hoped their friendship would develop.

When the Indians had driven or ridden off, Fielding heard Aziz call his name. He turned and went back into the bedroom. Aziz was sitting up in bed, looking miserable.

'Here's the famous hospitality of the East,' he said bitterly. 'Look at the paper coming off the walls. Look at the flies. Isn't it wonderful? I suppose you have to go now.'

'You want to rest, don't you?'

'I can rest the whole day. Before you go, will you please unlock that drawer? Do you see a photograph? Look at it.'

'Who is this?'

'She was my wife. She died. You are the only Englishman who has ever seen her. Now put her photograph away.'

Amazed, Fielding felt like a traveller who suddenly sees flowers between the stones of the desert. The flowers have been there all the time, but suddenly he sees them. He said, 'I don't know what I've done to deserve this, Aziz, but I do appreciate it.'

'Oh, it's nothing, she was not a highly educated woman or even beautiful, but I loved her. You would have seen her, so why not see her photograph?'

'You would have allowed me to see her?'

'Why not? I believe in the purdah, but I would have told her you were my brother. Hamidullah saw her, and several others.'

'Did she think they were your brothers?'

'Of course not, but the word exists and is convenient. All men are my brothers, and as soon as one behaves like my brother, he may see my wife.'

'And when the whole world behaves like your brother, there will be no more purdah?'

'It is because you can say and feel such a remark that I show you the photograph,' said Aziz seriously. 'It is beyond the power of most men. It is because you behave well when I behave badly that I show it to you. Mr Fielding, no one can ever realize how much kindness we Indians need, we do not even realize it ourselves. But we know when it has been given. We do not forget, though we may seem to. Kindness, more kindness, and even after that more kindness. It is the only hope.' His voice seemed to rise from a dream. 'We can't build up India except on what we feel.'

Fielding sat down by the bed, feeling rather sad and old. He wished he too could be carried away on waves of emotion. What had he done to deserve this confidence and what could he offer in exchange? He looked back at his own life. How dull *his* secrets were! He had been in love, engaged to be married, lady broke it off, memories of her had kept him from other women for a time, and now he was able to live calmly, without love. 'I shall never be really close to Aziz,' he thought, 'or to anyone.' And he had to confess that he didn't mind, that he was content to help people and like them as long as they didn't object, and if they objected, he would simply pass on by.

'How did you like the two ladies you met last Thursday?' he asked.

Aziz shook his head without replying; the question reminded him of his stupid remark about the Marabar Caves.

'How do you like Englishwomen generally?' continued Fielding.

'Hamidullah liked them in England. Here we never look at them. Oh no, we're much too careful to do that.'

'Hamidullah's right – they're much nicer in England. There's something that doesn't suit them out here.'

'Why don't you marry Miss Quested?' Aziz suddenly asked.

'Good Heavens! Certainly not! She depresses me.'

'But why? I thought her so nice and sincere.'

'She probably is,' said Fielding, ashamed of his roughness. 'But I can't marry her even if I wanted to, because she's just become engaged to the City Magistrate, Mr Heaslop.'

'Has she indeed? I'm so glad!' Aziz said with relief. This meant the Marabar expedition would come to nothing, because she would be Mr Heaslop's responsibility from now on. 'No Miss Quested for poor Mr Fielding! However, she is not beautiful. She has practically no breasts, when you come to think of it. For you, I shall arrange to find a lady with breasts like mangoes . . .'

'No, you won't.'

'I will not really, and besides, your position as head of Government College makes it dangerous for you.' Now he took up a new attitude towards his friend, the attitude of a protector who knows the dangers of India. 'You can't be too careful, Mr Fielding. I was a good deal upset when you talked in that way about God. Someone may report it. It was very unwise of you.'

'Thanks for telling me that. But what's the harm in it?'

'The result of it might be that you lose your job.'

'If I do, I shall survive. I travel light.'

'Travel light! You are a most extraordinary race. Is it your climate, or what?'

'Plenty of Indians travel light too, holy men and so on. Any man can travel light until he has a wife or children. That's part of my objection to marriage. I'm a holy man without the holiness.'

Aziz was charmed and interested. So this was why Mr Fielding was so fearless! He had nothing to lose. Aziz himself was tied by social and religious traditions which he could never break.

Still, now he and Fielding were friends, brothers. They trusted each other. Once the Englishman had left, Aziz fell asleep among the happier memories of the last two hours – a poem, visions of lovely women, Hamidullah, Fielding, and his respected wife.

PART TWO

Caves

The earth knows of a time when neither the River Ganges nor the Himalayas existed, but the Marabar Hills have been there since land began. They are older than anything in the world. Catching sight of them makes the visitor gasp; they rise suddenly, crazily out of the plain, unlike anything dreamt or seen before.

It is easy to describe the caves. A tunnel three metres long, two metres high and one metre wide leads to a large round cave, about seven metres across. This arrangement is found again and again in the Marabar Hills, and this is all, this is a Marabar Cave. Having seen one such cave, the visitor returns to Chandrapore uncertain whether he has had an interesting experience or a dull one or any experience at all. He finds it difficult to keep them apart in his mind, because the pattern never varies, and nothing, not even a cave drawing, distinguishes one from another.

They are dark caves. There is little to see, until the visitor strikes a match. Immediately another flame rises in the depths of the rock and moves towards the surface like an escaping spirit; the walls of the cave have been rubbed until they shine. The two flames approach and try to join, but cannot, because one of them breathes air, the other stone. The light increases, the flames touch one another, kiss and die. The cave is dark again, like all the caves.

The tunnel is an entrance, made by man. But deeper in the rock, are there other rooms which have no entrances? Local report declares that, just as there are more dead than living people, there are more hidden caves than open ones. It is believed that they are empty, so if they were discovered, nothing, nothing would be added to the total of good or evil in the world.

5
A visit to the caves

One evening at the club Miss Quested said to someone, 'An Indian I know, Dr Aziz, said he would arrange a little expedition for Mrs Moore and me. But he hasn't yet. Indians do seem rather forgetful.' She was heard by a servant, who reported it to Mahmoud Ali, and Aziz learnt with horror that the ladies were deeply offended with him. He felt obliged to organize the trip to the caves at once. He invited Fielding and old Godbole first, followed by the ladies. Then began a worrying few days of planning, to make sure that he could entertain these important guests in the best possible way, and that nothing would go wrong.

At last the day arrived. In order to be punctual, he had spent the previous night at the railway station, with the large number of servants he had hired or borrowed from friends, and with old Mohammed Latif, who was to be his assistant. A car drove up, containing Mrs Moore, Miss Quested, and their servant. Aziz rushed to meet them, suddenly happy.

'Oh, how very, very kind of you to come!' he cried. 'This is the happiest moment of my life.'

The ladies were polite. It was not the happiest moment of their lives; still, they looked forward to enjoying themselves as soon as they had recovered from the early start. They watched the servants running up and down the platform, putting food and equipment on to the train, and then they finally entered their private compartment.

Aziz was still on the platform, looking out for Fielding and

Godbole, when suddenly there was a short whistle and the train started moving. Aziz jumped on the train, but there were Fielding and Godbole, held up at the gates of the level crossing. Disaster! As the train slowly passed them, there was time for a few words.

'Bad, bad, you have ruined my plan!' cried Aziz.

'It was Godbole's prayer that did it,' shouted back Fielding. 'I had to wait while he finished it.'

'Jump on, I must have you,' screamed Aziz, holding out a hand. Fielding jumped, failed, missed his friend's hand, and fell back on the road. 'I'm all right, you're all right, don't worry,' he called after them, and then they heard his voice no more.

Aziz was almost crying with disappointment, but Mrs Moore said encouragingly out of the window, 'It will be a truly Muslim expedition now.' She was perfect as always, his dear Mrs Moore. He felt he would do anything, even die, to make her happy.

'We're going to have a delightful time without them,' called the other lady. Not perfect like Mrs Moore, but sincere and kind.

As the train continued its journey, Adela looked out at the dull fields, in the timeless half-darkness. She was feeling annoyed with herself. She could not understand why she was not more enthusiastic about seeing the 'real' India with Aziz, or about her engagement to Ronny. They were to be married in May, and arrangements were now being made for the wedding.

Mrs Moore was finding it hard to show much interest in the details of Ronny and Adela's wedding. Increasingly, she felt that, although people are important, their relationships are not, and in particular too much fuss has been made about marriage over the years – mankind is still no nearer to understanding mankind. Today she felt this opinion with such force that it seemed like a person who was trying to take hold of her hand. She was in rather low health, and had only agreed to come on the expedition as a companion for Adela, and quite soon she fell asleep.

When she awoke, Adela was watching the sun rising behind the huge grey Marabar Hills. The train slowed down and stopped at a small station, where an elephant was waiting. 'Oh, what a surprise!' called the ladies politely. Aziz said nothing, but he nearly burst with pride and relief. The elephant was the one grand part of the trip, and God alone knew how difficult it had been to obtain her. She belonged to the Nawab Bahadur, and Hamidullah Begum had a friend who was the mother of someone who knew the Nawab well. That an elephant should descend from so long and so delicate a string filled Aziz with contentment. 'Friends of friends are a reality in the East,' he thought, 'and sooner or later everyone gets his share of happiness.'

The elephant knelt, grey and lonely, like another hill, and the ladies climbed up a ladder on to its back, accompanied by Aziz and Mohammed Latif. As the elephant moved in a dignified way towards the hills, a strange, lifeless silence spread over the plain. Miss Quested asked questions about the hills, but no one knew the answers. Nothing was explained, and there was no real beauty to look at. Waves of heat coming off the rocks increased the visitors' confusion. As the elephant followed a path round the foot of the hills, suddenly the plain disappeared and nothing was to be seen on either side but steep walls of rock. The sky seemed unhealthily near, like a low ceiling.

Busy with his hospitality, Aziz noticed nothing. But his

guests did. They did not feel that it was an attractive place or quite worth visiting, and wished it could have become some interesting Muslim building, which their host would have appreciated and explained. His ignorance about the hills and the caves was evident.

The elephant stopped in the shadow of one of the hills, and here they camped. A cloth was laid on a folding table; tea and lightly boiled eggs were served to the ladies. Aziz had been warned that the English never stop eating, and that he should feed them every two hours. The ladies were impressed by his thoughtfulness, and he was grateful to them for allowing him to offer hospitality, which is what all Indians desire to do.

Adela was still thinking about her personal situation, and decided to ask Aziz's advice about it. 'I don't know whether you have heard,' she began, 'but I'm going to marry Mr Heaslop.'

'My warmest congratulations,' Aziz replied. His mind closed up against her, because she was marrying a British official.

'How can I avoid being, well, unpleasant to Indians, as so many Englishwomen are? That would make me very ashamed.'

'You are absolutely unlike the others, I can tell you. You will never be rude to my people.'

'I am told that we all get rude after a year.'

'Then you are told a lie,' he flashed back, because she had spoken the truth, and this seemed an insult in the circumstances. He recovered himself and laughed, but her mistake broke up their conversation. 'Come along,' he said, holding out a hand to each. They got up, a little unwilling to start their sightseeing.

To reach the first cave, they climbed over some unattractive stones, with the sun crashing on their backs, and disappeared one by one into a black hole in the rock. For Mrs Moore, it was

a horrible experience. The cave was crowded because the
servants had all come in too, and she nearly fainted. She lost
Aziz's hand in the dark, couldn't breathe, and felt something
strike her in the face. She tried to find the way out, but hit her
head. For a moment she went mad, hitting out and gasping like
a person drowning. Not only did the lack of air alarm her, there
was also a terrifying echo. In a Marabar Cave, whatever is said,
the same noise replies, echoing up and down the walls. It is a
dull sound like 'boum'. A sneeze, a polite word, a footstep, all
produce 'boum'.

When she was out in the daylight again, she felt a little better.
She realized that nothing evil had been in the cave, but she had
not enjoyed it, and decide not to visit a second one. Aziz was
not at all offended, and he and Miss Quested set off with a
guide to climb up to the next caves, while Mrs Moore rested in
a chair in the shade.

Mrs Moore took out her writing paper and began a letter to
her children in England. 'Dear Stella, dear Ralph,' she wrote,
then stopped. She looked around her at the forbidding rocks
and the opening to the cave. The more she thought about her
experience, the more frightening it became. The echo began in
some indescribable way to destroy her hold on life. Coming at
a moment when she felt weak and tired, it had managed to say
to her, 'Goodness and courage exist, but so does evil. They are
all the same.' She tried to continue her letter, reminding herself
that she was only an elderly woman who had got up too early
and journeyed too far, that even if she went mad the rest of the
world would go on. But suddenly, at the edge of her mind,
religion appeared, and she knew that all its holy words added
up to nothing more than 'boum'. Then she was truly terrified,
and found no comfort for her soul. She didn't want to write to

her children, or communicate with anyone, not even God. She sat stiff with horror, lost in her vision of complete despair.

High above her and out of sight, Miss Quested and Aziz were climbing up the steep path to the higher caves. From time to time Aziz took Miss Quested's hand to help her over the difficult places, while he thought about the large cooked meal which his servants should now be preparing for his guests. He had never liked Miss Quested as much as Mrs Moore, and had little to say to her.

Nor had Adela much to say to him. Her thoughts were with her marriage. She hoped it would be a happy one – luckily she and Ronny both had plenty of common sense. But as she climbed over a rock, she thought, 'What about love?' She and Ronny – no, they did not love each other. The discovery came so suddenly that she felt like a mountaineer whose rope has broken. Not to love the man one is going to marry! But soon she became calmer. 'If love were everything, few marriages would survive,' she thought.

'Are you married, Dr Aziz?' she asked, frowning.

'Yes, indeed, do come and see my wife.' He thought it better to have his wife alive for a moment.

'Thank you,' she said absently. 'And have you children?'

'Yes, indeed, three,' he replied in a firmer voice.

'Are they a great pleasure to you?'

'Naturally, I love them very much,' he laughed.

What a handsome little man he was! He did not attract her personally, but she guessed he might attract women of his level in Indian society. Probably he had several wives – Muslims always insisted on their full four, according to Mrs Turton. And having no one else to discuss marriage with, she said in her honest, reasonable way, 'Have you one wife or more than one?'

'Have you one wife or more than one?' asked Adela.

The question shocked the young man very much. To ask an educated, modern-thinking Indian Muslim how many wives he has – dreadful! 'One, one in my particular case,' he managed to say, and let go of her hand. There were a number of cave openings in front of them, and thinking, 'I hate the English,' he ran into one of them to recover his calm. She walked on more slowly, quite unaware that she had said the wrong thing. Not seeing him, she also went into a cave, thinking with half her mind 'sightseeing bores me', and wondering with the other half about marriage.

An unexpected arrest

Aziz waited in his cave a minute, and lit a cigarette. When he came out, he found the guide alone. He heard the noise of an engine, and by climbing on to a rock he could see a motor car coming towards the hills from Chandrapore. He climbed down to tell his guest the news. But the guide explained she had gone into a cave.

'Which one?' asked Aziz. The guide pointed uncertainly behind him. 'It was your duty to keep her in sight,' said Aziz. 'Here are at least twelve caves. Which cave was I in myself?' The guide clearly had no idea. There seemed to be caves in every direction, and all the openings looked the same. Aziz thought, 'Good Heavens, Miss Quested is lost,' and then recovered and began to look for her calmly. But the place was so confusing that it appeared impossible to find her. 'Come here,' he called to the guide, and when the man came close enough, hit him in the face to punish him. The man ran away, and Aziz was left alone. And then he discovered the simple explanation of the mystery.

Miss Quested wasn't lost. She had joined the people in the car, friends of hers, no doubt. For a second he caught sight of her far down the hill, standing between rocks, speaking to another lady. He was so relieved that he did not think her behaviour strange. He started to climb back down the hill to his camp, where Mrs Moore was, and almost at once he saw something lying at the entrance to a cave – Miss Quested's field-glasses, with a broken strap. He put them in his pocket.

Down on the plain he heard the car engine starting, but he couldn't catch sight of the car. He went on down the hill, and at last the colour and confusion of his little camp appeared, and in the middle of it he saw – oh joy! – a smiling Fielding.

'Fielding! Oh, I have so wanted you!' he cried, dropping the 'Mr' for the first time. And his friend ran to meet him, so pleasant and natural, shouting explanations. Fielding had come in the newly arrived car. That other lady was Miss Derek, who had met him by chance at the post office, heard how he had missed the train, and offered to drive him to the Marabar at once. Excellent Miss Derek!

But when Fielding heard that Miss Quested had left the expedition so unexpectedly, and, according to the servants, was at this moment on her way back to Chandrapore with Miss Derek, he felt sure that something was wrong.

Aziz spoke cheerfully, giving his own view of events. 'She ran to her friend, I ran to mine,' he said, smiling at Fielding and Mrs Moore. 'And now I am with my friends and they are with me, which is happiness.'

Loving them both, he expected them to love each other. They didn't want to. Fielding thought angrily, 'I knew these women would make trouble,' and Mrs Moore thought, 'This man, having missed the train, tries to blame us.'

'Perhaps Miss Quested was ill,' Fielding suggested to Aziz.

'She would have wanted me, as a doctor, to look after her.'

'Yes, that sounds sensible.'

'Let's talk of other things,' Aziz said kindly. 'I am glad that Miss Quested does what she wants. Don't worry for my sake.'

'I do worry for your sake. I consider she has been impolite,' said Fielding in a whisper. 'She had no right to go so suddenly.'

But today, talk of possible rudeness meant nothing to the

usually sensitive Aziz. The wings that held him high beat strongly, because he was a Mogul Emperor who had done his duty in the best tradition of Eastern hospitality. He had spent a small fortune on the expedition, and there had been huge difficulties to overcome, but he had given his guests as good a time as he could. And the arrival of his friend Fielding, whom he now began to think of as 'Cyril', had made his day complete.

The servants packed everything up. Mrs Moore and Fielding, followed by Aziz and Mohammed Latif, took their seats on the elephant, and soon they were at the little station. Mrs Moore went to her carriage, and the men went to theirs. Everybody tried to sleep on the train, but the heat was almost unbearable. At last they reached Chandrapore, and the trip was over.

And as they sat up in the train and prepared to enter ordinary life, suddenly the strangeness of the long morning broke. Mr Haq, the police inspector, threw open the door of the men's carriage and said loudly, 'Dr Aziz, it is my highly painful duty to arrest you.'

'Some mistake, I think,' said Fielding, at once taking control of the situation. 'What are you charging him with?'

'I am under instructions not to say, sir.'

'Very well, we'll find out. Come along, Aziz, old chap. Nothing to worry about. It must be a mistake.'

The young man sobbed – his first sound – and tried to escape out of the opposite door on to the railway line.

'That will oblige me to use force,' cried Mr Haq miserably.

'For God's sake!' cried Fielding, pulling Aziz back and shaking him like a child. A second later, and he would have been out, whistles blowing, the police chasing after him . . . 'My dear chap, we're going to the police station together, to find out what's gone wrong. Never, never act the criminal.'

'My children and my name!' he gasped, his wings broken.

'Nothing of the kind. Take my arm. I'll stay with you.'

They stepped out on to the platform, arm in arm. The station was crowded with passengers, British officials, and more police. Ronny took Mrs Moore away. Mohammed Latif began to sob. And before they could get through the crowd, Fielding was called away by the commanding voice of Mr Turton, and Aziz went on to prison alone.

Fielding was called away by the commanding voice of Mr Turton,
and Aziz went on to prison alone.

The Collector had watched the arrest from inside the waiting room, and throwing open its doors, he was revealed like a god in a shrine. When Fielding entered, the doors were closed and guarded by a servant, to mark the importance of the moment. Mr Turton could not speak at first. His face was white, stern and rather beautiful – the expression that all English faces would wear at Chandrapore for many days. Always brave and unselfish, he was now moved by a powerful emotion; he would have killed himself, obviously, if he had thought it right to do so. He spoke at last. 'The worst thing in my whole career has happened,' he said. 'Miss Quested has been insulted in one of the Marabar Caves.'

'Oh, no, oh no, no,' gasped Fielding, feeling slightly sick.

'She escaped – thank God.'

'Oh no, but not Aziz . . . it's impossible . . .'

'I called out to you just now to save you from being seen to accompany him to the police station. People would never forgive you for that,' said Mr Turton heavily.

Fielding felt that a cloud of madness had descended on them all, and he did not know how to fight it. 'Who makes this accusation?' he asked, trying to speak calmly.

'Miss Derek and – the victim herself . . .' Mr Turton nearly broke down, unable to say the girl's name.

'Miss Quested herself accuses him of—'

Mr Turton nodded and turned his face away.

'Then she's mad,' said Fielding.

'I cannot let that last remark pass,' said the Collector, trembling with anger. 'You will withdraw it instantly.'

'I'm awfully sorry, sir, I certainly do withdraw it.'

'Mr Fielding, what can have made you say such a thing?'

'The news gave me a very great shock, so I must ask you to

forgive me. I cannot believe that Dr Aziz is guilty. There is some mistake here, and in five minutes it can be put right.'

. 'There certainly is a mistake here,' came the thin, biting voice. 'I have had twenty-five years' experience of this country, and during that time I have never known anything but disaster result when English people and Indians try to become close friends. I have been Collector at Chandrapore for six years, and if everything has gone smoothly, it is because both races have kept to that simple rule. When newcomers depart from our traditions, you see what happens – in an instant all my work is undone, and the good name of my area ruined for years. I wish I had never lived to see this day, Mr Fielding. That a young lady engaged to my most valued official, an English girl fresh from England – that she—'

Involved in his own emotions, he broke down. What he said was both dignified and touching, but had it anything to do with Aziz? Nothing at all, if Fielding was right. It is impossible to see a disaster from two points of view, and while Turton hoped to get revenge for the girl, Fielding hoped to save the man. He was anxious to get away and talk to Mr McBryde, the Chief of Police, who had always been friendly to him, and was on the whole a sensible man.

'I meant to tell you,' added Mr Turton, 'that there will be a meeting at the club this evening to discuss the situation, but I am doubtful whether you will care to come.'

'I shall certainly come, sir, and I am grateful to you for informing me. May I ask where Miss Quested is?'

The Collector could hardly get the words out. 'She is ill.'

'Worse and worse,' said Fielding, with feeling in his voice.

But the Collector looked at him sternly, because he had not gone mad at the words 'an English girl fresh from England', he had not jumped to the defence of their race. He still wanted facts, though the rest of the English community had decided on emotion.

Closing the interview, Mr Turton walked out on to the platform. The confusion here was most unpleasant, with servants quarrelling and stealing the food and equipment from Aziz's expedition. The Collector understood the situation at a glance, and his sense of justice made him control his anger. He spoke the necessary word, and the stealing stopped. Then he drove off to his bungalow, still bitterly angry. When he saw Indians in the bazaars and in the streets, he thought, 'I know what you're like at last. You shall all pay a high price for this.'

7
Taking sides

Mr McBryde was the best educated of the Chandrapore officials. He had read and thought a good deal, and had decided that all natives were criminals at heart, because of the effects of their climate. So he was saddened but not surprised to hear of the accusation against Aziz. When Fielding arrived in his office, McBryde told him all he knew. Miss Derek and Miss Quested had arrived at his bungalow an hour before, in a terrible state, and he had arranged for Aziz's arrest at the station.

'What is he accused of, exactly?' Fielding asked.

'That he followed Miss Quested into the cave and came insultingly close to her. She hit at him with her field-glasses; he pulled at them, the strap broke and she ran away. And here's the evidence,' McBryde went on, showing Fielding the field-glasses with the broken strap. 'He had them in his pocket.'

'Did she say any more?'

'There was an echo which seems to have frightened her.'

'An echo? Did it upset her?'

'I couldn't worry her with too many questions. She'll get enough of those at the trial. I wish the Marabar Hills and all they contain were at the bottom of the sea.'

'I suppose there's no chance of my seeing Miss Quested?'

'I don't think she's well enough to see anyone. She's staying at my house for a while. My wife and the Callendars are taking care of her.'

'You see, I believe there's been a terrible misunderstanding, and that poor boy is innocent.'

The policeman looked surprised, and a shadow passed over his face. 'I had no idea that was in your mind,' he said.

'If he *had* tried to touch her,' said Fielding, 'he would never have put the field-glasses in his pocket.'

'Oh, that's quite possible, I'm afraid. When an Indian goes bad, anything can happen. You're a teacher, Fielding, and you meet these people at their best. They can be charming as boys. But I know them as they really are, after they've developed into men. Look at this, for example.' He held up Aziz's wallet. 'There's a letter here from a friend in Calcutta, arranging for him to see loose women there.'

'I don't want to hear about his private letters. And as for visiting loose women, I did the same at his age.'

So had the Chief of Police, but he did not want to admit it.

'Look here, old chap,' went on Fielding, 'if I see Miss Quested, there's a chance of her withdrawing the charge before it comes to court. I only want to ask her whether she's certain that it was Aziz who followed her into the cave.'

'Possibly my wife might ask her that much.'

'But I want someone who believes in him to ask her.'

'What difference does that make?'

'She is among people who don't trust Indians.'

McBryde said nothing, but reached for the telephone. 'I'll have to ask Major Callendar.' And a few minutes later came the expected answer: the patient could not be interviewed. 'He says she is by no means out of danger yet,' added McBryde.

They were silent. Two business cards were brought in, from Mahmoud Ali and Hamidullah, legal advisors to the prisoner. The opposite army was gathering.

'I can see your prisoner, I suppose,' said Fielding.

McBryde hesitated. 'What's the good? Why mix yourself up

with them? Whether he's innocent or guilty, why get involved?'

'I've got to do something!' cried Fielding desperately. 'I can't see *her*, and now I can't see *him*!'

'Look, old chap, you don't know this poisonous country as well as I do, so you must take it from me that the general situation at Chandrapore is going to be very nasty over the next few weeks.'

'I know that very well!'

'But at a time like this, there's no room for personal views. We have to hold the line against the enemy, and if you desert your own people, you leave a space in the line.' He pointed at the lawyers' cards. 'A space is just what *they* are looking for.'

'Can I see Aziz?' Fielding insisted.

'No. You will have to get a magistrate's order to see him.'

At this moment, more 'evidence' appeared – a desk-drawer from Aziz's bungalow, brought in by a policeman.

'Photographs of women. Ah!' said McBryde.

'That's his wife,' said Fielding unhappily.

With a disbelieving little smile, McBryde started looking through the drawer. 'Wife indeed, I know those wives!' he was thinking. Aloud he said, 'You'd better leave now, old man.'

Fielding found Hamidullah waiting outside the office. The Indian jumped up respectfully when Fielding greeted him.

'It's all a mistake!' cried Fielding passionately.

'Ah, ah, has some evidence come?' asked Hamidullah.

'It will come,' said Fielding, holding his hand.

'Ah yes, Mr Fielding, but once an Indian has been arrested, we do not know where it will stop. I appreciate your greeting me in this public manner, but nothing convinces a magistrate except evidence.'

Chandrapore's leading lawyer, with his dignified manner

and Cambridge degree, was seriously worried. He too loved Aziz and knew he was wrongly accused, but he spoke of 'evidence' in a way that saddened the Englishman.

Fielding, too, had his worries – he didn't like the field-glasses – but he put them to the back of his mind. At the moment when he was taking the Indians' side, he realized the great distance that divided him from them. Indians always do something disappointing, he thought. Aziz had tried to run away, Mohammed Latif had sobbed on the platform, and now Hamidullah was anxious about the defence. It is not that Indians are cowards, but fear is everywhere in India – British rule rests on it.

But Fielding managed to cheer Hamidullah up by telling him that Miss Quested would never be able to prove her accusation. They discussed who should defend Aziz at the trial; Hamidullah wanted Amritrao, a famous Calcutta lawyer, and although Fielding was worried about his anti-British reputation, he agreed that Amritrao would give Aziz the best chance of winning.

'I must go back to the College now,' he said. 'Goodbye, my dear Hamidullah (we must drop the "Mr" now). Give Aziz my love when you see him, and tell him to keep calm, calm, calm.'

'Goodbye, my dear Fielding, and you actually are on our side against your own people?'

'Yes, absolutely.'

Fielding regretted taking sides. He had hoped to creep through India without being identified in any way. From now on he would be called anti-British, and that would make him less useful. Things could become unpleasant.

Back at the College, he had a strange conversation with Professor Godbole. The professor had been speaking of other matters, then added, 'I am so glad that after all you succeeded in reaching the Marabar. I hope the expedition was successful?'

'The news has not reached you yet, I see. There has been a terrible disaster with our friend Aziz.'

'Oh, yes. That is all round the College.'

'Well, that means it can hardly be called a successful expedition,' said Fielding, with an amazed stare.

'I cannot say. I was not present.'

Fielding stared again, quite uselessly, because no eye could see what lay at the bottom of the Hindu's mind. 'I am most awfully upset about it,' he said.

'So I saw as soon as I entered your office. I will not take up your time much longer, but I would like your advice on a private matter. I am leaving the College soon, as you know, and returning to my birthplace at Mau, in Central India. I want to start a school there, which will be as like Government College as possible.'

'Well?' sighed Fielding, trying to take an interest.

'I hope to start more than one school, if possible.'

Fielding sank his head on his arms. Really, Indians were sometimes unbearable.

'My question is this,' continued Godbole. 'What name should be given to the school?'

'A name for a school? I am sorry, I have no names for schools in my head. I can think of nothing but our poor Aziz. Do you understand that he is at the present moment in prison?'

'Oh yes. I had thought of the "King George Fifth School".'

'Godbole! Is Aziz innocent or guilty?'

'That is for the court to decide.'

'Yes, yes, but your personal opinion. Did he do it or not?'

'You are asking whether an individual is likely to do good or evil, and that is difficult to say. Good and evil are both part of our world. God is present in one, and absent in the other. That is why we say to God, "Come, come." But did you have time to visit any of the interesting Marabar ruins?'

Fielding was silent, trying to rest his brain. The professor went on to tell a charming story about a Hindu Rajah and the Marabar Hills, but Fielding could not bring himself to reply.

In the afternoon he obtained permission and visited Aziz in prison, but found him unapproachable through misery. 'You deserted me,' were the only words that Fielding could understand. He went away to write a letter to Miss Quested. Even if it reached her, it would do no good, and probably the McBrydes would keep it from her. It did surprise him that the accusation came from her. She was such a dry, sensible person, and so open-minded; the last person in Chandrapore to accuse an Indian wrongfully.

Although Miss Quested had not previously been popular with the English, she now brought out all that was fine in their character. 'What can we do for our sister?' was the only thought of the women as they drove to the McBrydes' to enquire. Mrs Turton was the only visitor allowed into the patient's room. She came out shining with an unselfish sorrow. 'She is my own darling girl,' were the words she spoke, and then, remembering that she had called her 'not pukka', she began to cry. No one had ever seen the Collector's wife cry; she had always reserved her tears for some great occasion, and now it had come.

People drove calmly into the club that evening – the natives must not suspect they were alarmed. One young mother, a brainless but most beautiful girl, sat on a sofa in the smoking room with her baby in her arms; her husband was away and she dared not return to her bungalow, in case 'the natives attacked'.

As the wife of a minor official, she was usually snubbed, but today she represented all that was worth fighting and dying for.

'Don't worry, my dear,' said Mrs Turton, standing protectively over her like a goddess of war, 'you'll be safe at the Collector's bungalow – that's where you and your baby will sleep tonight.'

The Collector clapped his hands for silence, and made a short speech, directed at the ladies. They must all stay calm, very calm. The accused was safely locked up in prison. The drums they could hear in the bazaars were just part of the normal preparation for the Indian festival of Mohurram, and nothing to worry about.

The ladies were asked to leave the smoking room, and the men began to discuss the situation in more detail. They started speaking of 'women and children' – each man felt that all he loved best in the world was in danger, and demanded revenge on Indians in general. A young army officer, who was visiting the club that evening, said the army would have to be called in.

Just as the talk was getting heated, the door opened and Mrs Turton called out, 'She's better,' and a general sigh of joy and relief was heard. Major Callendar, who had brought the good news, came in.

'Can't promise anything,' he growled. 'No one's out of danger in this country if they have a temperature. I've found out a bit more about the attack, though. Heaslop had told Miss Quested's servant not to lose sight of her. Prisoner got his friend Mohammed Latif to bribe the servant to stay behind. And what about the Englishman, our friend here?' He glanced at Fielding. 'How did they get rid of him? Money again.'

Fielding rose to his feet, supported by murmurs and exclamations. For the moment, no one suspected his honesty.

'Oh, I'm being misunderstood, apologies,' said the Major offensively. 'I didn't mean they bribed Mr Fielding.'

'Then what do you mean?' asked Fielding.

'They bribed the other Indian, Godbole, to make you late.'

Fielding sat down, trembling with anger. Just then the door opened again, and Ronny came in.

The young man looked exhausted, and seemed to appeal for their protection. Out of respect for him and his suffering, they rose to their feet. But all behaviour is political in India, and while supporting him, they were dismissing Aziz and India. So Fielding remained seated. This was noticed by Major Callendar, who called out, 'The prisoner has one of his friends here.'

'Mr Fielding, what has prevented you from standing up?' asked the Collector coldly. It was the attack which Fielding had been waiting for, and he must reply to it.

'May I make a statement, sir?'

'Certainly.'

Fielding stood up and said simply, 'I believe Dr Aziz to be innocent. I shall wait for the court's decision. If he is guilty, I resign from my post and leave India. I resign from the club now.' He started moving towards the door.

'One moment, Mr Fielding,' said the Collector. 'Before you leave the room, you will express some disgust at the crime, and you will apologize to Mr Heaslop.'

'Are you speaking to me officially, sir?'

The Collector, who never spoke in any other way, became so furious that he lost all control. 'Leave this room at once! You have sunk to the level of your friends! You—'

'I want to leave, but am being prevented,' said Fielding lightly. The army officer was standing solidly in front of the door.

'Let him go,' said Ronny, almost in tears. It was the only appeal that could have saved the situation. Whatever Heaslop wished must be done. The officer moved away from the door.

Fielding left the room, and stood for a moment on the veranda, looking out at the Marabar Hills. At this distance and this hour they were beautiful. What criminal was hidden there? What was the 'echo' which the girl complained of? He must find out.

Because he was thinking hard, he did not notice the perfect moment when night descended and the hills disappeared. He felt suddenly doubtful and disappointed, and wondered whether he was really successful as a human being. He had learnt to make the best of his life, according to advanced European rules. But now he felt he ought to have been working at something else the whole time – he didn't know what, never would know, never could know, and that was why he felt sad.

8
Doubts

Adela lay for several days in the McBrydes' bungalow. She had been touched by the sun, and hurt herself on the rocks as she had rushed downhill towards Miss Derek's car. People were kind to her, indeed too kind, the men respectful, the women sympathetic, but Mrs Moore, the only visitor she wanted, kept away. She often relived the experience: 'I went into this hateful cave, and then the echo started, and then there was a shadow blocking the entrance. I hit at him with my glasses, he pulled me round the cave by the strap, it broke, I escaped, that's all. He never actually touched me once. It all seems such nonsense.' Then her eyes always filled with tears. 'Naturally I'm upset, but I'll get over it.' And then she would break down completely, and the women would cry too, and the men in the next room would murmur, 'My God, my God!'

If only she could have seen Mrs Moore! The old lady had not been well either, Ronny reported. The echo was still there in Adela's head. The sound had followed her out of the cave and was still going on, like a river gradually flooding the plain. Only Mrs Moore could drive it back to its cave and block the entrance. Evil was present – she could hear it entering the lives of others. And Adela spent days in this atmosphere of misery and depression.

When her cuts had healed and her temperature fallen to normal, Ronny came to collect her. He looked tired and pale, and she wished she could comfort him, but it seemed easier to talk of facts than feelings. He told her there had been trouble

*'I went into this hateful cave, and then the echo started,
and then there was a shadow blocking the entrance.'*

during the Mohurram festival, when the procession left its official route and approached the English bungalows. However, McBryde and his police had managed to prevent any violence.

Ronny also told her about the trial. She would have to appear in court, identify the prisoner, and be questioned by an Indian lawyer.

'Can Mrs Moore be with me?' was all she said.

'Certainly, and I'll be there myself,' Ronny replied. 'Das, my assistant, will be the magistrate. They've objected to me because I'm too involved, they say. But he's a good chap, intelligent in his way. Oh, and there's a letter for you from Fielding. I hope you don't mind, but we opened it when you were ill. I'm afraid the defence have got hold of him and he's on their side now.'

'What does the letter say?' she asked weakly.

'It's not worth thinking about. He says the man is innocent, and suggests you might have made a mistake.'

'I wish I had! But think of Mr Fielding's behaviour to you at the club, Ronny, when you already had to bear so much for my sake! That was shocking of him. Well, let's go, let's go.'

Mrs McBryde, a woman she had nothing in common with, wished her a warm goodbye. They would have to meet now, year after year, until one of their husbands retired. Truly, British India had caught Adela in the trap she had tried to avoid.

Ronny drove her home, and as the bungalow came in sight, he said, 'Mother's looking forward to seeing you, but of course she's old, you mustn't forget that.' He seemed to be warning her about a possible disappointment, but Adela felt sure that her friendship with Mrs Moore was so deep and real that it would last, whatever else happened. 'You'll find her a little bad-tempered,' he added. 'Well, we all are at the moment.'

They found Mrs Moore sitting on a sofa. She didn't get up as they entered, and only said, 'Here you are both back.' Adela sat down and took her hand, but Mrs Moore withdrew it. 'I've been looking at my return ticket,' the old lady said. 'I would like to go home to England immediately after your wedding.'

'We can discuss that later,' said Ronny crossly. 'Now, how do you think our Adela is looking?'

'I rely on you to help me through. It's wonderful to be with you again. Everyone else is a stranger,' said the girl rapidly.

But Mrs Moore showed no desire to be helpful.

'There is this echo that I keep on hearing,' continued Adela.

'Oh, what about the echo?' asked Mrs Moore, looking at her for the first time.

'I can't get rid of it.'

'I don't suppose you ever will.'

'Mrs Moore, what is this echo? Do say! I felt you would be able to explain it – that would comfort me so—'

'If you don't know, you don't know. I can't tell you.'

'I think you're rather unkind not to say.'

'Say, say, say,' said the old lady bitterly. 'I have spent my life saying or listening. It is time I was left in peace. When I've seen you and Ronny married, and seen my other two children and whether they want to be married – then I'll retire into a cave of my own. Somewhere where no young people will come asking questions and expecting answers.'

'I hope you're not going to talk like that when you're giving evidence at the trial,' said her son hotly.

'I'll have nothing to do with your laughable law courts,' she replied angrily. 'I refuse to give evidence. All this rubbish about love, love in a church, love in a cave, as if there is the least difference!' She got up slowly and left the room.

Ronny turned to Adela and found, as he expected, that the poor girl was crying. And as always, there was a servant outside the window, listening. Much upset, Ronny sat silent for a moment, wishing he had never asked his mother to visit India.

'I'm sorry, my dear girl,' he said, 'this is a poor welcome home for you. I never realized she felt like that.'

Adela had stopped crying. An extraordinary expression was on her face, half relief, half horror. 'Aziz, Aziz.' It was the first time she had said his name. 'Aziz . . . have I made a mistake?'

'You're overtired,' he cried, not much surprised.

'Ronny, he's innocent. I made an awful mistake.'

'Sit down anyway.' He looked round, but could see no one listening, and he took her hand.

She suddenly touched her ear and gasped, 'My echo's better! Ronny, dear Ronny, help me to do the right thing. Aziz is good. You heard your mother say so.'

'Mother never said that. She never mentioned his name.'

'But Ronny, I heard her. When she talked about love, at the end she said, "Dr Aziz never did it." Well, perhaps it was the idea more than the words.'

'No, my dear girl, his name wasn't mentioned by anyone. Look here, you're confusing this with Fielding's letter.'

'Oh, that's it, that's it!' she cried, greatly relieved.

'So you won't say he's innocent again, will you? Every servant I've got is a spy.' He went to the window again, and found just two small children there – impossible that they should know English, but he sent them away.

Mrs Moore returned to the room with a pack of cards, and sat down at the card table. To end the confusion, Ronny asked her if she had mentioned the prisoner. She replied, 'I never said his name,' and began to lay the cards out on the table.

'I thought you said, "Aziz is innocent",' Adela said.

'Of course he is innocent,' she replied, without looking up.

'You see, Ronny, I was right,' said the girl.

'You weren't right, she never said it.'

'But she thinks it.'

'Who cares what she thinks?'

'Is it again my duty to talk?' asked Mrs Moore crossly.

'Only if you have anything sensible to say,' replied her son.

'Oh, how dull, how unimportant it all is!' Her voice seemed to come from a great distance and out of darkness. 'When shall I be free from your fuss? Was he in the cave and were you in the cave and on and on . . . and ending everything the echo.'

'You send it away,' said Adela. 'You do nothing but good.'

'I am not good, no,' she spoke more calmly. 'A bad old woman, bad. I met a young man in his mosque, I wanted him to be happy. Happiness is a dream . . . But I will not help you to poison his whole life for what he never did. There are different ways of evil and I prefer mine to yours.'

'Have you any evidence for your belief in his innocence?' asked Ronny, in his magistrate's voice. 'If so, it is your duty to speak in his defence in court. No one will stop you.'

'I know his character,' said his mother dismissively, 'and it isn't the kind of thing he would do.'

'That is hardly evidence, mother.'

Adela said, 'It would be so dreadful if I was wrong.'

He turned on her and said, 'Don't listen to my mother. You know you're right, and the whole community knows it too.'

'Yes, but – this is very, very awful. I'm as certain as ever that he followed me – only, wouldn't it be possible to withdraw the charge? I hate the idea of giving evidence more and more. Oh, of course, it's out of the question, please forgive me.'

'That's all right,' he said awkwardly. 'The case has to come before a magistrate now – it must, the machinery has started.'

'She has started the machinery,' said Mrs Moore from the card table. 'It will work to its end.'

Adela started crying again as a result of this unkind remark, and Ronny had an excellent idea. His mother ought to leave India at once; she was doing no good to herself or anyone else.

The next day he contacted the steamship company, but all the tickets were sold for several months ahead. Fortunately, however, Lady Mellanby, the Lieutenant-Governor's wife, came to the rescue, offering the old lady a place in her own cabin. It was like a gift from heaven, and Ronny was very grateful.

So Mrs Moore had all she wished. She escaped the trial, the wedding, and the hot weather. At her son's suggestion and her own desire, she departed. But she accepted her good luck without enthusiasm. The echo had affected her deeply. What had spoken to her in that cave? Something very old and very small, something that lived before time and before space – evil itself. Since hearing its voice, she had not had one beautiful or generous thought.

However, as the train which carried her to Bombay rushed across Central India, she began to look out and wonder at the scenery, just as she had done when she first arrived in the country. 'I have not seen enough of India,' she thought despairingly. But now it was too late. Soon she was on the ship, watching the coast of India disappear, and listening to Lady Mellanby's advice to go to the cabin, to shelter from the sun.

9
The trial

On the morning of the trial, Adela was on her knees in her bedroom. After years of ignoring religion, she had recently started praying again; it was the shortest and easiest way to the unseen, and she could include her troubles in her prayers.

'Are you ready, young lady?' called Mrs Turton. Adela had been staying with the Turtons since Mrs Moore's departure, and they had been extremely kind to her. But no one, not even Ronny, knew what her real feelings were. In her sadness she had said to him, 'I bring you nothing but trouble. I was right that evening at the polo, we had better just be friends.' But he had protested; the more she suffered, the more highly he valued her. Did she love him? she wondered. Was she capable of loving anyone?

She came out into the hall. 'I am sure to break down,' she said nervously, 'but I think I'll get my verdict, don't you?'

'You're certain to win,' said Mr Turton calmly, and did not tell her there would be unpleasantness whatever the verdict was. The Nawab Bahadur had paid for the defence, and would face financial ruin rather than let 'an innocent Muslim die'. The atmosphere of the city was changing. As the Collector's car turned into the street, there was a tap of silly anger on the side of the car – a stone thrown by a child. Several native police on motor bicycles arrived, and rode on either side of the car through the bazaars.

'How unnecessary,' murmured the Collector. 'McBryde's making too much fuss.'

But Mrs Turton said firmly, 'A show of force will do no harm, Harry – it's silly to pretend they don't hate us.'

He replied sadly, 'I don't hate them, I don't know why,' and thought to himself, 'After all, it's our women who make everything more difficult out here.'

They reached Ronny's private room at the courthouse, where Ronny, Miss Derek, Major Callendar, and McBryde were waiting. They discussed the street cleaners who had refused to work today, in support of Aziz, and the Muslim ladies who had declared they would not eat until he was released. No one quite understood what was happening, but they decided that Fielding was to blame for it all, and they spoke fiercely against him. He had been seen driving up with the accused's two lawyers, Amritrao and Mahmoud Ali.

Miss Quested took no part in their discussion, but lay back in her chair with her eyes closed, reserving her strength. They noticed her after a while, and felt ashamed of making so much noise.

'Can't we do anything for you?' asked Miss Derek kindly.

'I don't think so, thank you, Nancy.'

When the case was called, servants entered the court first, carrying chairs for all the English officials. It was important for the English to look dignified, and when everything was ready for them, they walked in and sat down in a group at the front.

The court was very crowded and very hot. The first person to speak was the Chief of Police, opening the case for the prosecution. Adela sat calmly, listening to McBryde, and wondering for what purpose she had collected this roomful of people together.

The accused, said McBryde, was a man of loose life, who had carefully planned his attack on the victim. Then he could not resist adding, as a scientific observation, that while the dark-skinned races are physically attracted by the fair-skinned ones, this does not happen the other way round.

'Even when the lady is so much uglier than the gentleman?'

The comment fell from nowhere, and Mr Das, the magistrate, sitting up on his platform, felt obliged to react.

Adela sat calmly, wondering for what purpose she had collected this roomful of people together.

'Send that man out,' he said nervously. A policeman took hold of a man who had said nothing, and pushed him roughly out of the room. But the remark had upset Miss Quested, and Miss Derek asked her if she felt faint. Her friends began to fuss around her, and Major Callendar called out, asking the magistrate if Miss Quested could sit on the platform, to benefit from the fresher air there. When this was agreed, the whole English group followed Adela up on to the platform, once the servants had rearranged their chairs.

But the famous lawyer from Calcutta, Amritrao, got to his feet. 'We object to the presence of so many English ladies and gentlemen on the platform,' he said in his Oxford-educated voice. 'They may appear threatening to the witnesses.'

'Forget about the trial and let's have the verdict,' growled the Major.

The magistrate pretended he hadn't heard this. 'I agree to the objection,' he said, hiding his face in some papers. 'Miss Quested's friends should kindly step down from the platform.'

'Well done, Das,' said Ronny, with surprising honesty.

The case continued. Miss Quested felt better, and felt sure she would come through all right. She passed the good news on to Mrs Turton and the Major, but they were too angry about the attack on British pride to be interested. Mr Das was also happier, having won the battle of the platform.

At the end of McBryde's speech, he stated that the accused had made his servants crowd into a cave which another English lady had entered, in order to get rid of her and leave him free for his crime. These words brought on a storm of cries and shouts among the Indians present, and Mahmoud Ali, who was assisting Amritrao, became furious. He screamed like a madman, asking whether the accused was charged with murder as well. McBryde replied that he was not calling the other English lady as a witness.

'You can't, because you have taken her secretly out of the country! She is Mrs Moore, she would have proved the prisoner's innocence, she was on our side, she was poor Indians' friend!'

'Neither side has called her, neither side can use her as evidence,' cried the magistrate desperately.

'She was kept from us until too late – this is English justice! Give us back Mrs Moore for five minutes only and she will save my friend, she will save the name of his sons! Mr Das, help us, as you yourself are a father! Tell us where they have put her, oh, Mrs Moore—'

'This is no way to defend your case,' advised the magistrate. 'As a witness Mrs Moore does not exist.'

But it was all too much for Mahmoud Ali. 'This trial is unjust, because of the British – I am going!' And he handed his papers to Amritrao and left, calling passionately from the door, 'Aziz, Aziz, goodbye for ever!' The noise in the room increased, and Mrs Moore's name could now be heard outside, shouted out by the crowds as a kind of magic spell, *'Esmiss Esmoor, Esmiss Esmoor, Esmiss Esmoor . . .'*

Eventually, Mr Das brought the court back to order, and by the time Adela came to give her evidence, the atmosphere was quieter than it had been since the beginning of the trial.

She had always meant to tell the truth and nothing but the truth. The only difficulty was that the disaster in the cave was connected to another part of her life, her engagement to Ronny. She had thought of love just before she went in, and had innocently asked Aziz about marriage. She supposed that her question had made him think about her in that way. She was determined not to speak about this, her private failure, but to be completely honest about everything else.

However, as soon as she heard the sound of her own voice, she lost her fears, and felt protected by a new and unknown feeling. She didn't need to use her memory to answer questions, because she had returned to the Marabar Hills, and spoke from them across a sort of darkness to Mr McBryde. Every detail was there, the train, the sun, the elephant, the first cave, Mrs Moore's tiredness. Why had she thought the expedition dull? It was beautiful now. Smoothly McBryde's voice went on in the distance, leading her along the paths of truth . . .

'The prisoner and the guide took you up to a group of caves?'

'Yes.' She saw the steep-sided rock, felt the heat on her face.

'You went alone into one of those caves?'

'That is quite correct.'

'And the prisoner followed you.'

'Now we've got him,' came from the Major.

She was silent. The court was waiting for her reply. But she could not give it until Aziz entered the cave.

'The prisoner followed you, didn't he?' repeated McBryde. He and Adela had practised these questions and answers before, so this part of the trial held no surprises.

'May I have half a minute before I reply to that?'

'Certainly.'

Her vision was of several caves. She saw herself in one, and she was also outside it, watching to see if Aziz entered. She failed to see him. It was the doubt that had often visited her, but solid and attractive now, like the hills.

'I am not—' Speaking was more difficult than seeing. 'I am not quite sure.'

'I am sorry, what did you say?' asked McBryde.

'I cannot be sure . . .'

'I didn't catch that answer.' He looked frightened. 'You have entered a cave. I suggest to you that the prisoner followed you.'

She shook her head.

'What do you mean, please?'

'No,' she said in a flat voice. Slight noises began around the room, but no one yet understood what was happening, except Fielding. He saw that she was going to have a nervous breakdown and that his friend was saved.

'What is that, what are you saying? Speak up, please.' The little magistrate was bending forward.

'I'm afraid I have made a mistake.'

'What kind of mistake?' asked Das.

'Dr Aziz never followed me into the cave.'

The Chief of Police threw his papers on the desk, then picked them up and said calmly, 'Now, Miss Quested, let us go on. I will read you the words of your statement—'

'Excuse me, Mr McBryde, you cannot go on. I am speaking to the witness myself. And the public will be quiet, or I'll have the court cleared. Miss Quested, I am the magistrate dealing with the case, kindly direct your remarks to me. Be aware what an extremely serious matter this is. Remember you have sworn to tell the truth, Miss Quested.'

'Dr Aziz never—'

'I stop this trial as Chief Medical Officer! Miss Quested is too ill to continue!' cried Major Callendar, at a word from Turton. All the English rose from their chairs at once, large white figures behind which the little magistrate was hidden.

'You withdraw the charge? Answer me!' screamed the representative of justice.

Although Adela's vision was over, and she was back in the dull, ordinary world, she had learnt something from it. 'I withdraw everything,' she said.

'Mr McBryde, do you wish to continue?' asked Das.

The Chief of Police stared at Adela, asking, 'Are you mad?'

'Sahib, you will have to withdraw!' shouted the Nawab Bahadur suddenly from the back of the court.

'He shall not,' shouted Mrs Turton against the rising noise. 'Call the other witnesses – we're none of us safe—'

Ronny tried to speak to her, and she hit out at him angrily, then screamed insults at Adela. McBryde nodded casually to Das, 'Right, I withdraw.'

Mr Das rose, nearly dead with anxiety. He had shown that an Indian can keep control, just. To those who could hear him, he said, 'The prisoner is released without one stain on his character. The question of costs will be decided elsewhere.'

And then the noise and confusion became unbearable. People screamed and swore, sobbed and kissed each other. Here were the English, protected by their servants, and there was Aziz, fainting in Hamidullah's arms. Victory on this side, defeat on that. But gradually person after person struggled out of the room, and peace finally descended on the courtroom again.

10

Rescue

Miss Quested had cut the connection with her own people. Turning away from them, she was swept along with the crowd of Indians towards the public exit of the court. They did not notice her, but shook hands over her shoulder and shouted through her body. Without any purpose in the world she had created, she was accidentally thrown against Mr Fielding.

'What do you want here?' he asked.

Knowing him for her enemy, she passed on into the sunlight without speaking.

He called after her, 'Where are you going, Miss Quested? You can't wander about like that. Where's the car you came in?'

'I shall walk.'

'What madness – it's dangerous in the streets. No one knows what'll happen next. Why don't you keep to your own people?'

'Ought I to join them?' she said, without emotion. She felt emptied, valueless; there was no more goodness in her.

'You can't, it's too late, you can't reach the private exit now. Come this way with me – quick – I'll put you into my carriage.'

He pushed a way to the edge of the crowd. Behind them, Aziz's supporters had lifted him on to their shoulders, and were carrying him in a procession along the main street. The noise and confusion increased by the second.

'Cyril, Cyril, don't leave me,' called the broken voice of Aziz.

'I'm coming back,' Fielding called to him. 'This way, and don't argue,' he said to Adela, taking her arm. 'Send my carriage back any time tomorrow.'

'But where am I to go in it?'

'Where you like. How should I know your arrangements?'

The carriage was safe in a back street, but Fielding's servant had led the horses away, not realizing the trial would be over so soon. Adela got into the carriage obediently. Fielding could not leave her, because he feared for her life, in the increasing confusion that he could hear outside the courthouse.

'What have you been doing?' he cried suddenly. 'Playing a game, studying life, or what?'

'Sir, these are for you, sir,' interrupted a student, running towards Fielding with an armful of flowers. 'Sir, let us be your

'Cyril, Cyril, don't leave me!' called the broken voice of Aziz.

horses, sir,' cried his friends, as they joined him. And in spite of
Fielding's protest, they pulled the carriage down the street,
where it joined Aziz's victory procession. Their appearance
caused yet more confusion. Many people did not recognize
Adela when they saw her sitting next to Fielding, and they
cheered, some calling her Mrs Moore; flowers were put round
the necks of both of them. Others said, 'Look at the English,
always together!' It was a critical remark that Fielding himself
agreed with, and he knew that if by some misunderstanding an
attack was made on the girl, he would be obliged to die in
her defence. He didn't want to die for her, he wanted to be
celebrating with Aziz.

Where was the procession going? To friends, to enemies, to
Aziz's bungalow, to the Collector's bungalow, to Delhi. The
students decided they wanted to go to Government College, so
they turned away from the main procession, and ran the
carriage down a hill and through a gate into the mango garden
of the college. There, as far as Fielding and Miss Quested were
concerned, all was peace and quiet. The students rushed away
to fetch more of their friends.

Fielding took Miss Quested into his office and tried to
telephone McBryde, but found the wires had been cut. Once
more he was unable to desert Adela. He gave her a couple of
rooms, provided her with ice and drinks and some dry cake,
advised her to lie down, and lay down himself – there was
nothing else to do. He felt restless and annoyed as he listened to
the faint sounds of the procession, and his joy was spoilt by
puzzlement. It was a victory, but such a strange one.

At that moment Aziz was crying, 'Cyril, Cyril . . .' Crowded
into a carriage with the Nawab Bahadur, Hamidullah,
Mahmoud Ali, his own little boys, and a heap of flowers, he

was not content. He wanted to be surrounded by all who loved him. Victory gave no pleasure, he had suffered too much. From the moment of his arrest, he had dropped like a wounded animal; he had despaired, not through lack of courage, but because he knew that an Englishwoman's word would always outweigh his own. All that existed in that terrible time was his friends' love, and love for his friends was all that he felt in the first painful moments of his freedom. 'Why isn't Cyril following? Let us turn back.' But the procession could not turn back. It advanced like a snake down the narrow street towards the open space of the sports ground, where it would finally turn, and decide who or what to attack.

'Forward, forward!' screamed Mahmoud Ali. 'Down with the Collector, down with the Chief of Police!'

'This is not wise,' advised the Nawab. He knew nothing would be gained by attacking the English, and moreover he had great possessions and approved of the rule of law.

'But some little show of force is necessary,' said Hamidullah, 'or they will think we are still afraid of them.'

'Down with the Chief Medical Officer! To the Minto Hospital! Rescue the patients!' cried Mahmoud Ali, confusing the hospital with a prison. 'The English are mistreating Nureddin!'

The Nawab was shocked to hear the name of his grandson, who was in hospital recovering from a car accident, but he said firmly, 'I will not have my grandson made an excuse for an attack on the hospital. I saw him last week and he was in good health.'

However, Mahmoud Ali's words carried the crowd to new heights of anger, and they advanced on the Minto Hospital. Fortunately, there was no sign of Major Callendar, and his assistant, Dr Panna Lal, hurried to do what the protestors wanted. When Nureddin came out, with his face wrapped in bandages, there was a roar of relief. The Nawab took this opportunity to make a moving speech about justice, courage, and freedom, which cooled the passion of the crowd. He further announced that he would no longer be known as the Nawab Bahadur, which is what the British called him, but plain Mr Zulfiqar, and he invited his friends to a victory dinner at his country house that evening.

Now that the excitement was over, people began to go back to their homes. The heat was increasing, and before long most of the residents of Chandrapore, on both sides of the divide, were asleep.

☙

Fielding had hoped, when he woke up, to find that someone had taken Miss Quested away, but she was still there and clearly wanted to talk.

'Have you any explanation of my extraordinary behaviour?' she asked.

'None,' he said coldly. 'Why make such a charge if you were going to withdraw it? I ought to feel grateful to you, I suppose—'

'I don't expect that. I only thought you might care to hear what I have to say. Wouldn't it interest you to hear my side?'

'Not much,' he replied rather rudely.

'The echo in my ears has gone,' the girl went on. 'You see, I have been unwell ever since that expedition to the caves, and possibly before it.'

This remark interested him; it was what he had sometimes suspected. 'One of three things happened in the Marabar,' he said. 'Either Aziz is guilty, which is what you and your friends think, or you invented the charge, which is what my friends think, or you had a hallucination. I rather think, now that you tell me you were unwell, that you yourself broke the strap of the field-glasses; you were alone in that cave the whole time.'

'Possibly. It could have been the sort of hallucination that makes some women think they've had an offer of marriage when none was made.'

'You describe it honestly, anyway.'

'The trouble is, being honest gets me nowhere.'

Liking her better, he smiled and said, 'It'll get us to heaven. If heaven existed.'

'Don't you believe in heaven, Mr Fielding?' she said shyly.

'I do not. But what a temptation, at my age, to pretend that the dead live again!'

'Because the dead *don't* live again.'

'I fear not.' There was a moment's silence.

'What does Dr Aziz say of me?' she asked.

'He – he's very bitter, naturally,' said Fielding awkwardly. Aziz's remarks about her were not just bitter, they were extremely unpleasant, for example, 'It disgusts me to be mentioned in connection with such a hag.' To avoid further questions about Aziz, Fielding added quickly, 'But there's a fourth possibility – was it the guide? Unluckily, we haven't been able to find him.'

'Perhaps it was the guide,' she said quietly. The question had suddenly lost interest for her.

At that moment Hamidullah joined them, and seemed not too pleased to find them together. He had come to take Fielding to the victory dinner at the Nawab's house.

'Miss Quested has been explaining her behaviour today,' said Fielding, who wanted the atmosphere to be friendly.

'Yes,' said Adela nervously. 'The fact is that I realized before it was too late that I had made a mistake, and had just enough sense to say so. That is all my extraordinary behaviour involves.'

'All it involves, indeed!' replied the Indian furiously. 'You blacken my best friend's name, damage his health and ruin his career in a way you cannot imagine, because of your ignorance of our society and religion, and then suddenly you say you are not quite sure, and he can be released. And now I understand you have not quite finished with us – you are accusing the poor old guide who took you to the caves.'

'We were just discussing possibilities,' said Fielding.

'There are one hundred and seventy million Indians in India, and of course one of them entered the cave. Of course some Indian is the criminal, we must never doubt that! And since, my dear Fielding, these possibilities may take some time' – he put an arm round the Englishman's shoulder – 'don't you think you had better come to the Nawab's house with me now? Or should I say to Mr Zulfiqar's, as he wants us to call him from now on?'

But Fielding still had to solve the problem of what to do with Miss Quested, and in spite of Hamidullah's protests, felt he had to allow her to stay at the College under his protection, for a few days at least. He had a natural sympathy for anyone who was miserable, and a new-found respect for her honesty and sincerity.

They were still discussing the problem when Hamidullah, who was standing at the window, saw a carriage arrive.

'Well, here's our solution,' he said. 'Here comes the City Magistrate, travelling in a closed carriage for secrecy.'

But Ronny had no solutions. He had a short interview with

Adela, in which she learnt that the English community had turned against her, and no one would offer her a room. He also told her that he had just heard of his mother's death, on board the steamship. She had been buried at sea.

Adela, who was very fond of Mrs Moore, was deeply upset by this last piece of news, and Fielding realized that, now more than ever, he could not turn her away. He arranged for his servants to look after her, and left her at the College.

As Hamidullah drove Fielding away in his carriage, he thought how silly and weak the Englishman had been, in helping Miss Quested out of her difficulty. But he said nothing. Instead he asked Amritrao, who was accompanying them, what amount Miss Quested ought to pay in compensation to Aziz.

'Twenty thousand rupees,' came the answer.

The remark horrified Fielding. He couldn't bear to think of the strange, honest girl losing her money and possibly her young man too. And, tired by the merciless and enormous day, he lost his usual sensible view of human beings, and felt that we exist not in ourselves, but in other people's minds – an idea which he had had only once before, the evening after the disaster, when from the veranda of the club he saw the fists and fingers of the Marabar Hills swell until they included the whole night sky.

11

The effects of the trial

'**A**ziz, are you awake?' asked Fielding.

'No, so let us have a talk. Let us dream plans for the future.'

The victory dinner was over, and the guests lay on beds on the flat roof of plain Mr Zulfiqar's large house in the country, looking up at the stars.

'Are you content with our day's work, Cyril?' Aziz continued.

'Are you?' said Fielding.

'Except that I ate too much. I say, Major Callendar will lose his job, I think.'

'Yes, some people will leave Chandrapore,' said Fielding.

'And you'll get promotion,' Aziz said.

'They can't very well get rid of me, whatever their feelings.'

'Anyway, you and I are going to spend our holidays together, and visit Kashmir, possibly Persia, because I shall have plenty of money. Paid to me for the injury to my reputation,' he explained with a small smile.

'You have won a great victory—' began Fielding.

'I know, my dear chap, I know. Your voice need not become so anxious. I know what you are going to say next. Let, oh, let Miss Quested off paying, so that the English may say, "Here is a native who has actually behaved like a gentleman; if it wasn't for his black face we would almost allow him to join our club." Their approval no longer interests me, I have become anti-British, and ought to have done so sooner – it would have saved me many misfortunes.'

'Including knowing me.'

'I say, shall we go and pour water on Mohammed Latif's face? He is so funny when this is done to him asleep.'

The remark was not a question but a full stop. There was a pause, pleasantly filled by a little wind which managed to brush the top of the house.

Fielding tried again. 'Yes, certainly, you must let off Miss Quested easily. She must pay all your costs, that is only fair, but do not treat her like a defeated enemy.'

'Is she wealthy? I order you to find out.'

'The amounts mentioned at dinner when you all got so excited – they would ruin her. Look here—'

'I *am* looking, although it gets a bit dark. I see Cyril Fielding to be a very nice chap indeed and my best friend, but in some ways not very wise. You think that by letting Miss Quested off easily I shall make a better reputation for myself and Indians in general. No, no. The English will say it's weakness and an attempt to gain promotion for myself. I have decided to have nothing more to do with British India, actually. I shall find a post in a Muslim state, where Englishmen cannot insult me any more. Don't try to advise me against it.'

'During a long talk with Miss Quested—'

'I don't want to hear about your long talks.'

'Be quiet. During a long talk with Miss Quested, I have begun to understand her character. She is perfectly sincere and very brave. When she saw she was wrong, she said so. Do you realize what that meant? All her friends around her, the whole of British India pushing her forward. In her place I wouldn't have had the courage. Do treat her kindly. I know what all your friends want,' – he nodded at the figures on the other beds around them – 'but you mustn't listen to them. Be merciful, like one of your great Mogul Emperors.'

'Not even Mogul Emperors showed mercy until they received an apology,' said Aziz.

'She'll apologize if that's the trouble,' cried Fielding, sitting up. 'Look, tell me what you want her to say. I'll write it all down, and tomorrow I'll bring it back here, signed by her. That would be in addition to any public apology, of course.'

'How about "Dear Dr Aziz, I wish you had come into the cave; I am an awful old hag, and it was my last chance." Will she sign that?'

Fielding sighed, and lay down again. 'Well, after that, it's time to go to sleep. Good night.'

'Good night.' Then after a few moments' silence, Aziz added, in a voice that was dreamy and full of feeling, 'Cyril, I have an idea which you will like. I shall ask Mrs Moore.' He did not know that she was already dead, as his friends had not wanted to spoil the victory celebrations by telling him. 'Her opinion will solve everything – I can trust her absolutely. She has my best interests at heart, unlike you. If she advises me to pardon this girl, I shall.'

'Let us discuss that tomorrow morning.'

'I keep forgetting that she has left India. I shall have to write. She is now far away, well on her way towards Ralph and Stella.'

'To whom?'

'To her other children. Didn't you know of them? Just as I have two boys and a girl, so has Mrs Moore. She told me at the mosque. Oh, Mrs Moore! I have only met her three times, but I know she is truly one of us – she belongs to the East.'

'You are so unreasonable . . . you won't treat Miss Quested generously, while for Mrs Moore you have extreme respect. At least Miss Quested did the right thing this morning, but the old lady never did anything for you at all. And it's just a guess as to whether she would have come forward on your side at the trial.'

'You do not like Mrs Moore, and are annoyed because I do. However, you will come to like her eventually.'

When a person, really dead, is supposed to be alive, the conversation becomes awkward. Fielding could not bear it any longer, and burst out, 'I'm sorry to say Mrs Moore's dead.'

But Hamidullah, who had been listening to all their talk, and did not want the evening spoilt, cried from the next bed, 'Aziz, he is joking. Don't believe him.'

'I do not believe him,' said Aziz calmly. He was used to all sorts of practical jokes, even of this type.

Fielding said no more. Facts are facts, and Aziz would learn of Mrs Moore's death in the morning. But it made him realize that people are not really dead until they are felt to be dead.

Mrs Moore had become ill soon after leaving Bombay, had died on the ship, and was buried at sea. Behind her, she left some discomfort, because a death gives a ship a bad name. Lady Mellanby did all that was required and more, because she was a kind woman. But a Lieutenant-Governor's wife does not expect to have such an experience, and she hardly knew the elderly lady who had died in her cabin.

The death took on more lasting shapes in Chandrapore. A rumour began to spread that an Englishman had killed his mother for trying to save an Indian's life, and there was just enough truth in this to cause annoyance to the Collector and his officials. At one time it was reported that there were two shrines to Mrs Moore's memory, but quite soon the general interest in her died away.

Ronny reminded himself that his mother had left India at her own wish, but he still felt partly responsible, at least for her early departure from India. He knew he had behaved badly towards her, but how annoying she had been, with her admiration for Aziz! What a bad influence on Adela! And now she was still giving trouble, with these shrines, mixing herself up with natives. The young man had much to worry him – the heat, the local unrest, the approaching visit of the Lieutenant-Governor, the problems of Adela, and the unwelcome publicity surrounding his mother's death. What does happen to a mother when she dies? Probably she goes to heaven; anyway she is no longer there. Wherever he entered, mosque, cave or temple, Ronny's views on religion remained the same – it was something a chap shouldn't talk about too much. He dismissed the matter from his mind. After a while he and Stella and Ralph would pay for a stone to be placed in the churchyard of his mother's church in England, recording the dates of her birth and death and the fact that she was buried at sea. That would be quite enough.

And Adela – she would have to depart too. He had hoped she would suggest it herself before now. He really could not marry her; it would mean the end of his career. Poor Adela – she remained at Government College, through Fielding's kindness, but none of the English would receive her. He put off all private talk until Aziz's claim for compensation had been decided. Then he would ask her to release him from the engagement. She had killed his love, which had never been very strong. They would never have got engaged if it hadn't been for the accident in the Nawab Bahadur's car.

12

Departure from India

The visit of the Lieutenant-Governor took place in the next few days. Sir Gilbert Mellanby had modern ideas. His long career in government had protected him from personal contact with the people of India, so he was able to speak of them in a civilized way, and to criticize racial prejudice. He approved of the trial verdict, and congratulated Fielding on taking 'the sensible, the only possible view' from the first. Speaking confidentially, he told Fielding that the matter had been 'mismanaged by certain of our friends up the hill', who did not realize that 'the hands of the clock move forward, not back' and so on and so on. One thing he could promise: the headmaster would receive a warm invitation to rejoin the club, and Sir Gilbert begged, no, commanded him to accept. The Lieutenant-Governor left Chandrapore well satisfied; how much Miss Quested would have to pay, what exactly had happened in the cave – these were local details, and did not concern him.

Fielding found himself more and more involved with Miss Quested's problems. He ate and slept at Hamidullah's, so she stayed on in her rooms at the College. A house to live in, a garden to walk in during the few moments of coolness – that was all she asked, and he was able to provide it. Disaster had shown her her limitations, and he realized now what a fine character she had. She never complained of getting the worst of both worlds, but saw it as the punishment she deserved for her stupidity. He helped her to write a letter apologizing to Aziz, but they both realized there was something wrong with it.

'Our letter is a failure, for the simple reason that you have no real feeling for Aziz, or for Indians generally,' said Fielding. 'The first time I saw you, you were wanting to see India, not Indians, and I knew that wouldn't take you very far. Indians know whether they are liked or not – they cannot be deceived about that. Justice never satisfies them – they want more than that, they want affection – and that's why all our work in India rests on sand.'

Then she said, 'Do I like anyone, though?' Fielding assumed she liked Heaslop, and changed the conversation, as this side of her life did not concern him.

Victory had made Fielding's Indian friends rather aggressive. They wanted to develop their attack on British rule, and kept discovering new insults and wrongs, many of which were invented. Although Sir Gilbert had been most polite to them, the system he represented had in no way bowed its head. British officials were still there, as constant and unpleasant as the sun, and what was to be done about them was not very obvious, even to Mahmoud Ali.

Aziz was friendly and persuasive. He wanted Fielding to 'become part of the East', as he described it, and depend wholly on the society of Indians for affection and friendship. 'You can trust me, Cyril.'

No question of that, and Fielding had no reason to stay with his own people, but he really couldn't become a sort of dependent poor relation, like Mohammed Latif. When they argued about it, some racial difference seemed to come between them. And Aziz would finish, 'Can't you see that I'm grateful to you for your help and want to reward you?' And Fielding would reply crossly, 'If you want to reward me, let Miss Quested off paying.'

Aziz's insensitiveness about Adela displeased Fielding, and one day he had the idea of appealing to the memory of Mrs Moore. Her death had been a real sorrow to the Indian's warm heart; he sobbed like a child, and ordered his three children to cry too. There was no doubt that he respected and loved her. Fielding's first attempt was a failure. Aziz's reply was, 'I see your trick. But I want revenge on the English. Also I want the money – to educate my little boys.' But he began to weaken, and whenever the question of compensation was discussed, Fielding mentioned the dead woman's name. Aziz gave in quite suddenly. He felt it was Mrs Moore's wish that he should spare the woman who was going to marry her son, and, in a passionate and beautiful speech, he sacrificed the whole of the compensation money, claiming only his costs.

It was fine of him, and as he expected, it won him no respect from the English. They still believed he was guilty; they believed it to the end of their careers. And retired majors in quiet English towns still murmur to each other about the Marabar trial which went so badly wrong because the poor girl could not face giving her evidence.

When the matter was officially ended, Ronny, who was being transferred to a post away from Chandrapore, came to see Fielding at Hamidullah's house. He politely thanked Fielding for the help and hospitality he had given Miss Quested. 'I understand she would like to see you,' he added.

Fielding went to the College at once, and found her rather upset. He learnt that the engagement had been broken by Ronny.

'Far wiser of him,' she said miserably. 'I ought to have spoken myself, but I just went on, wondering what would happen. I have become a public nuisance without realizing it.' In order not to make him anxious, she added, 'I speak only of India. Don't think I shall do harm in England, I'll be all right there. I have enough money, and lots of friends of my own type. But, oh, the trouble I've brought on everyone here – my carefulness about whether we should marry or not – and in the end Ronny and I part and aren't even sorry. We should never have thought of marriage. Weren't you amazed when our engagement was announced?'

'Not much. At my age I'm seldom amazed,' he said, smiling. 'Marriage is a crazy idea, anyway. I have friends who can't remember why they married, and neither can their wives.'

'I'm not against marriage, but – I entered that cave, thinking, "Am I fond of him?" I haven't told you that before, Mr Fielding. Friendship, respect, I tried to make them take the place of—'

'I no longer want love,' he said, providing the word.

'Neither do I. But I want others to want it.'

'But to go back to our first talk, when you entered that cave, who did follow you, or did no one follow you? Can you say?'

'Let us call it the guide,' she said, with little interest in her voice. 'It will never be known. There was something there that neither of us can understand. Mrs Moore – she did know.'

'How could she have known what we don't?'

'She had a feeling for atmosphere. Perhaps she felt what was happening. I don't know. It doesn't seem likely, does it?'

'No, but I agree with you, there could be something outside the limits of our knowledge that we will never really understand.' He smiled at her. 'Write to me when you get to England.'

'I shall, often. You've been extremely kind. I wish I could do something for you in return, but I see you've got all you want.'

'I think I have. I've never felt happier out here. I really do like Indians, and they trust me. Until the next earthquake I remain as I am.'

'Of course, Mrs Moore's death made me very unhappy.'

'Aziz was so fond of her too.'

'But it has made me remember that we must all die. The idea that death spares no one begins to be real.'

'Don't let it become too real, or you'll die yourself. I want to go on living for a while.'

'So do I,' she agreed.

A friendliness was in the air. Both man and woman were at the height of their powers – sensible, honest and intelligent. They spoke the same language and held the same opinions, but in some way they were dissatisfied. The shadow of a shadow of a dream fell over them, like a faint message from another world.

'And I do like you so very much, if I may say so,' he said.

'I'm glad, because I like you. Let's meet again.'

'We will, in England, if I ever get a holiday.'

'But I suppose you're not likely to do that yet.'

'Actually there's quite a chance of it happening soon.'

'Oh, that would be very nice.'

Ten days later Adela went off, by the same route as her dead friend. Her last Indian adventure was with her servant, who followed her on to the boat and demanded money from her in return for his silence. Mr Fielding had been her lover, the servant said. She rang the cabin bell and had him taken off the ship, but he repeated his statement about her in public, and the other passengers did not speak to her much during the voyage.

Another local result of the trial was a better understanding between Hindus and Muslims, and this had an effect on Aziz's plans for the future. In a conversation with Hamidullah, he said, 'I shall go right away from here.'

'Where to? Turtons and Burtons, all are the same.'

'I want to get away from British India, even to a poor job. My idea now is to try for a post as a doctor in one of the Hindu states. I may be able to write poems there.'

'But the money, the money – those Rajahs will never pay a reasonable salary.'

'I shall never be rich anywhere, it is not in my character to be rich.'

'If you had been sensible and made Miss Quested pay—'

'I chose not to. Discussion of the past is useless,' he said, with a sudden sharpness. 'I have allowed her to keep her fortune and buy herself a husband in England. She will need all her money for that. Don't mention the matter again.'

'Very well, but your life must continue a poor man's. No holidays in Kashmir for you now. You must work, and study, and make English doctors respect you, so that you get promotion and a high salary, not retire to a Hindu state to write poems.'

'There are many ways of being a man,' said Aziz calmly. 'Mine is to express what is deepest in my heart.'

'There is no reply to that,' said Hamidullah, moved. Then he added, smiling, 'Have you heard this naughty rumour that Mohammed Latif has got hold of? When Miss Quested stayed at the College, Fielding used to visit her – rather too late in the evening, the servants say.'

'A pleasant change for her if he did,' said Aziz. 'Still, that does not help me out of my difficulty. I am determined to leave Chandrapore.' Suddenly, surprising both Hamidullah and himself, he lost his temper. 'Who is there to help me? No one is my friend. I have had enough of friends. All betray me, even my own children.'

'I was going to suggest we go behind the purdah, but your three children, who have betrayed you, are there, so you won't want to.'

'I am sorry. Ever since I was in prison, my temper has been strange. Take me there, forgive me.'

And Aziz went behind the purdah, to see his children. They had come for the trial, and had stayed on with Aziz's aunt, Hamidullah Begum. He spent a pleasant hour with them, eating the sweets his aunt made, called Elephants' Ears, and for the moment he was able to forget the rumour about Fielding that Hamidullah had just told him.

13

A rumour

Aziz had no sense of evidence. It was his emotions which decided his beliefs, and this led to the coolness between himself and his English friend. Fielding had gone away to a headmasters' meeting, so could not be questioned about his relationship with Miss Quested, and after a few days Aziz assumed the rumour was true. He had no objection to his friends amusing themselves, and Cyril, at his age, could no longer expect the best of the female market, and must take his amusement where he could find it. But why choose this particular woman, whom Aziz still considered his enemy?

He met Fielding at the railway station on his return, agreed to have dinner at the College with him, and then, in Fielding's carriage, started talking about the shocking news of Mr McBryde and Miss Derek. McBryde had been caught in Miss Derek's bedroom, and his wife was divorcing him.

'That pure-minded man,' said Aziz. 'However, he will blame the Indian climate. Everything is our fault really. But look here, Cyril, there's talk about you as well as McBryde. They say that you and Miss Quested also became rather too close friends, and in fact were guilty of immorality together.'

'They *would* say that. Who cares?'

'Imagine my anxiety. It's all over the city and may injure your reputation. I've done all I could to silence such a rumour.'

'Don't worry about it, my dear chap. It's not important. Remember, I travel light.'

'Cyril, boasting about travelling light will be your ruin. It is making you enemies everywhere. You observe I speak in a low voice. Every third servant is a spy.'

'That simply doesn't affect me,' said Fielding, smiling.

In the end Aziz was obliged to try a more direct approach. 'So you and Miss Adela used to amuse each other in the evenings, naughty boy.'

Fielding was so surprised that Aziz had taken the rumour seriously, and so disliked being called a naughty boy, that he lost his temper and cried, 'For God's sake! You little fool! Amuse each other, indeed! Is it likely, at such a time?'

'Oh, I'm sorry. It was the Indian imagination at work,' he answered cheerfully, but he was cut to the heart by the mistake he had made, and by Fielding's reply.

'You see, Aziz, the circumstances . . . also the girl was still engaged to Heaslop, also I never felt—'

'Yes, yes, but you didn't contradict what I said, so I thought it was true. Oh dear, the difference between East and West! Will you please put your little fool down at his hospital?'

'You're not offended?'

'Most certainly I am not. I believe absolutely what you say, and there need be no further question of it.'

'But the way I said it – I was unintentionally rude. I do apologize.'

'The fault is completely mine.'

Difficulties and misunderstandings like these still interrupted their conversations. Fielding began to explain again his feelings about Miss Quested, but Aziz interrupted.

'Oh, I believe you. Mohammed Latif just invented it.'

'We'll discuss that at dinner tonight,' said Fielding.

Aziz's eyes went hard. 'Dinner. This is most unlucky – I forgot. I have promised to have dinner with Das.'

'You are coming to dinner with me as arranged,' said Fielding firmly. 'I won't put up with your making any excuses. Make sure you come.'

They reached the hospital, and Fielding drove on alone in his carriage. He was annoyed with himself, but relied on dinner to mend his relationship with Aziz. At the post office he saw the Collector.

'Good morning. So you're back,' said Turton icily. 'I would be glad if you would come to the club this evening.'

'I have accepted your invitation to rejoin, sir. I would prefer not to come tonight, as I have arranged to have dinner with someone.'

'It is not a question of your feelings, but of the Lieutenant-Governor's wish. Perhaps you will ask whether I speak officially. I do. I shall expect you this evening at six.'

He attended the unpleasant little ceremony as requested. He was given a drink, he talked to McBryde about his divorce, he met the new Chief Medical Officer and the new City Magistrate, but the more the club changed, the more it looked certain to become the same thing.

'It's no good,' he thought, as he drove past the mosque on his way home, 'the British are building on sand. And the more modern the country gets, the worse the crash will be. Everything echoes now; there's no stopping the echo. The original sound may be harmless, but the echo is always evil.'

At dinner, he found Aziz overtired and depressed. He told Aziz about his visit to the club. 'But I won't go there again, unless Turton orders me to. And that means probably never, because I'm going to England quite soon.'

'I thought you might end in England,' Aziz said very quietly, then changed the conversation.

'I am only going for a short time, on official business.'

'Will your business leave you much spare time?'

'Enough to see my friends.'

'You are a good friend to have. I suppose you will visit Miss Quested.'

'If I have time. It will be strange seeing her in London.'

'There she lives in comfort. You will enjoy seeing her. Oh dear, I've got a headache this evening – perhaps it's a fever. With your permission I'll leave early.'

'When would you like my carriage?'

'Don't bother – I'll go by bicycle. I hear people say I am seen too often in your carriage.'

Their conversation was awkward; although they had strong feelings for each other, they did not think in the same way. As Aziz got up to leave, Fielding made one last effort to put the misunderstanding behind them.

'Aziz, have you forgiven me the stupid remark I made this morning?'

'When you called me a little fool?'

'Yes, to my great shame. You know how fond I am of you.'

'That is nothing. Of course, we all make mistakes. In a friendship such as ours, a few little things like that are of no importance.'

But as he drove off in Fielding's carriage (he had no bicycle at the College), something depressed him – a dull pain of body or mind, waiting to rise to the surface. When he arrived at his bungalow, he sat down miserably on his bed and stared at the flies on the ceiling. The trouble rose to the surface now. He was suspicious; he suspected his friend of intending to marry Miss Quested for the sake of her money, and of going to England for that purpose.

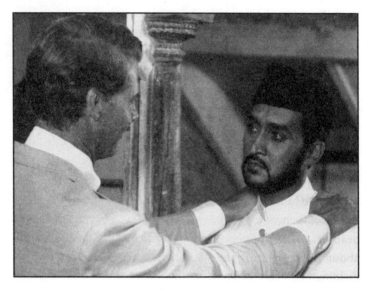

'Aziz, have you forgiven me the stupid remark I made this morning?'
said Fielding.

Being an Indian, he was able to trust and mistrust the Englishman at the same time. Fielding had saved the girl twenty thousand rupees in compensation, and now followed her to England. If he desired to marry her, all was explained; she would bring more money to the marriage. Cyril had surely been the girl's lover while she was staying at the College. But was that all? Perhaps it was Cyril who had followed her into the cave . . . No, impossible, he had not been there then. But the idea left him trembling with misery. Such a betrayal, if true, would be the worst in Indian history. He was shaken, as though he had been told a true fact.

Next day he decided to take his three children away from Chandrapore, back to their grandmother's home. They had come for the trial, to say goodbye in case he went to prison, and had stayed on at Hamidullah's for the celebrations. During his absence Fielding would go off to England, and future events would prove whether Aziz's suspicions were right.

Fielding was conscious that something was wrong, and his usual confidence failed him because he was really fond of Aziz. Travelling light is less easy as soon as feelings are involved. He wrote Aziz a letter about his views on women and morality, but Aziz did not care for it at all, and replied coldly, regretting his inability to see Fielding before the steamship sailed.

And Fielding went, and Aziz's suspicions became beliefs. His friends encouraged them, because, although they liked the headmaster, they felt uncomfortable that he now knew so much about their private lives. Mahmoud Ali soon declared that Fielding had betrayed Aziz, and Hamidullah warned Aziz 'not to expect too much, because he and she are, after all, both members of another race.'

Where are my twenty thousand rupees? thought Aziz. He had never cared about money, but those rupees were constantly on his mind, because he had allowed them to escape overseas, like so much of the wealth of India. Cyril would marry Miss Quested – he grew certain of it. It was the natural result of that horrible, senseless expedition to the Marabar, and before long he persuaded himself that the wedding had actually taken place.

PART THREE

Temple

Hundreds of miles west of the Marabar Hills, and two years later in time, Professor Godbole stands in the presence of God. God is not born yet – that will occur at midnight – but He has also been born centuries ago, nor can He ever be born, because He is the Lord of all Worlds, who is above and separate from human lives. He is, was not, is not, was. He and Professor Godbole stood at opposite ends of the same piece of carpet.

> *Tukaram, Tukaram,*
> *You are my father and mother and everybody . . .*

The carpet was in the courtyard of a palace, which belonged to the elderly Rajah of Mau. The Professor stood at one end, and at the other end was a shrine to Shri Krishna, the God who would be born at midnight.

Hindus were crowded into the courtyard, or temple, talking and laughing noisily, while waiting for the main event of the religious year. The professor was singing a holy song, and while he was singing, the picture of an old Englishwoman he had met at Chandrapore came into his mind. But as he was overcome by the excitement of the moment, she disappeared.

Just then a way was cleared through the crowd, and the ancient Rajah was carried in, to witness the birth ceremony. Suddenly the clock struck midnight. Loud music was played, red powder was thrown in the air, and in the rosy dust and shouting, Perfect Love took the shape of Shri Krishna, and saved the world. All sorrow was removed, not only for Indians, but for foreigners, birds, caves, railways and the stars; all became joy, all laughter; there had never been disease or doubt, misunderstanding, cruelty, fear.

In his arms the professor held a cloth in the shape of a baby. He gave it to the Rajah, who said, 'I name this child Shri Krishna.' Then his servants carried the Rajah away to his private rooms, where his doctor, Aziz, was waiting for him.

In his mind the professor saw Mrs Moore again, surrounded by a troubled atmosphere. She seemed to need his help, and it was his duty, and his desire, to speak to God for her. 'Come, come, come, come,' he said to Shri Krishna.

'That is all I can do,' he thought, as he stepped out of the temple into the grey of a rainy morning, 'and it is not much.'

14

The end of a friendship

D r Aziz left the palace later that day. As he returned to his house – which stood in a pleasant garden further up the main street of the town – he was thinking of Fielding. The Englishman had been transferred from Chandrapore, and sent on a tour through Central India to see what the more distant states were doing about English education. He had written to Professor Godbole announcing that he would be spending two days in Mau, inspecting the professor's new school. His wife and her brother would be with him.

But Aziz had no wish to see him again. Fielding had married; he had done the expected with Miss Quested. When still in Chandrapore, Aziz had received a letter from Fielding in London. Mahmoud Ali was with Aziz at the time. The letter said, 'Some news that will surprise you. I'm going to marry someone you know . . .'

Aziz said bitterly, 'Here it comes, answer for me,' and threw the letter to Mahmoud Ali. He destroyed later letters unopened. It was the end of a foolish experiment. And although sometimes at the back of his mind he felt that Fielding had made sacrifices for him, it was now all confused with his very real hatred of the English. 'I am an Indian at last,' he thought, standing still in the rain outside the temple.

Life passed pleasantly in Mau. The climate was healthy, so the children could be with him all year round, and he had married again – not exactly a marriage, but he liked to consider it one. He read his books, wrote his poems, and rode his horse in the jungle. His poems were all about Indian womanhood. 'The purdah must go,' they said, 'or we shall never be free.'

He had little difficulty adjusting to living in a Hindu state. He had no religious curiosity, and never discovered the meaning of the different festivals, but Professor Godbole had been most helpful in explaining details of daily life to him. He was now accepted by all in Mau as the Rajah's personal doctor, and head of the small hospital. The British kept an eye on Aziz – they had no evidence against him, but Indians who have been unfortunate must be watched, and to the end of his life he remained under observation, because of Miss Quested's mistake. He was unaware of this.

Yes, all had gone well so far, but now he had received a note from the professor, saying that Fielding and his companions were already in Mau, staying at the visitors' guesthouse, and were hoping to see something of the festival. Furiously Aziz tore the note up. He had had enough of showing Miss Quested native life. Ugly, hateful hag! He hoped to avoid them altogether if possible.

That morning Aziz took his children for a walk to a shrine on top of a nearby hill. While the children were playing on some rocks, he noticed Fielding, and someone who looked more of a boy than a man, climbing the hill to the shrine. Suddenly the boy cried out in pain; an insect had stung him.

It was impossible to avoid speaking to them. 'Good morning, gentlemen, can I help?' shouted Aziz. He went over to the stranger, and pulled the sting out of his wrist.

'How are you, Aziz, after all this time?' Fielding asked. 'Why haven't you answered my letters?' But then the clouds opened, and the sheets of rain sent the whole group hurrying downhill to the English people's carriage. Fielding tried to make conversation, but Aziz was determined not to be friendly. Fielding felt quite angry by the time they reached the carriage.

'Jump in, Mr Quested, and Mr Fielding,' said Aziz.

'For God's sake, who is Mr Quested?'

'Do I mispronounce that well-known name? Is he not your wife's brother?'

'I'm only Ralph Moore,' said the boy, reddening. Aziz tried to withdraw, but it was too late.

'Quested? Quested? Don't you know that my wife was Mrs Moore's daughter? Perhaps this explains your strange attitude?'

'And what is wrong with my attitude?'

'The awful letter you let Mahmoud Ali write for you. How could you make such a mistake? I wrote to you five or six times, mentioning my wife by name. Miss Quested! What an extraordinary idea!' From his smile, Aziz guessed that Stella was beautiful. 'Miss Quested is a friend of ours, but . . . This is Mahmoud Ali's fault. He knows perfectly well I married Miss Moore. He called her Heaslop's sister in his rude letter to me.'

The hated name made Aziz furious. 'So she is, and this is Heaslop's brother, your family now. What does it matter to me who you marry? I don't want you, I don't want any of you in my private life – with my dying breath I say it. Yes, I made a foolish mistake. I thought you married my enemy. I thought you'd stolen my money, but I forgive Mahmoud Ali for deceiving me, because he loved me.' He turned away. Cyril followed him through the mud, apologizing, laughing a little. But for Aziz it made no difference – he had built his life on a mistake, but it was too late to change it now. Speaking in Urdu, so that his children could understand, he said, 'Please don't follow us, whoever you marry. I wish no Englishman or Englishwoman to be my friend.'

Meanwhile the festival was continuing at the temple, and a large procession was beginning to gather in the street outside. An hour or two later, Aziz rode past on his way to the guesthouse. He had decided to take some medicine to rub on Ralph's sting, and anyway his horse needed exercising. His route passed the great lake of Mau, and out on the water he could see a small black shape, which he identified as the guesthouse boat. 'Ah!' he thought with disgust. 'Another attempt to "see India"!' The visitors clearly wanted to approach the temple from the lake, for a better view of the procession.

He continued on to the guesthouse, and entered what seemed an empty building. He looked curiously into room after room, and was rewarded by finding two letters on the piano. He was not ashamed to read them. After all, McBryde had read all his letters at Chandrapore. One was from Heaslop to Fielding, apologizing for his lack of friendliness on Fielding's marriage to his sister, and sending his best wishes to Adela. The other was from Miss Quested to Mrs Fielding, wishing the Fieldings a good trip round India. It was all 'Stella and Ralph', even 'Cyril' and 'Ronny' – all so friendly and sensible. He envied the easy relationships between men and women that are only possible in a nation where the women are free.

Something moved in the next room, and a voice called out nervously, asking who was there. Aziz slipped the letters into his pocket. 'State doctor, come to enquire, very little English,' he said.

Ralph Moore came into the light.

What a strange-looking boy, tall, the blue eyes anxious, the hair thin and untidy! Aziz thought. 'Come here, please, allow me to look.' He took the boy's hand roughly in order to examine the insect sting.

'Your hands are unkind,' said Ralph nervously.

Aziz realized the boy was right, but replied angrily, 'This is a most strange remark. I am a qualified doctor. I won't hurt you.'

'I don't mind pain – there is no pain.'

'Excellent news,' replied Aziz with an unpleasant smile.

'But there is cruelty. Dr Aziz, I have done you no harm.'

'Aha, you know my name, I see. Of course, your great friend Miss Quested did me no harm at the Marabar.'

Drowning his last words, all the palace guns were fired. Aziz and Ralph went on to the veranda. They could hear singing from the temple, and see lights moving all over the town.

'I must leave now, good night,' said Aziz, and held out his hand, completely forgetting that they were not friends. Then he remembered how unpleasant he had been, and said gently, 'Don't you think me unkind any more?'

'No.'

'How can you tell, you strange creature?'

'It's not difficult. It's the one thing I always know.'

'Then you are one of us.' He gave a little gasp as he remembered that these were the words he spoke to Mrs Moore at the mosque. Never be friends with the English, he had told himself. And here he was, starting again. He handed the medicine to Ralph. 'Take this and think of me when you use it. I must give you one little present – you are Mrs Moore's son – and it is all I have got. Did your mother speak to you about me?'

'Yes, in her letters. She loved you.'

'Yes, your mother was my best friend in all the world.' He was silent for a moment, puzzled by the strength of his feeling. 'How I wish she could have seen our rainy season! That is now, of course. You see the people out there, they are all joyful and happy, with their wild noise, although we cannot follow them because they are Hindus – they sing, they dance, and this is India. Oh, I wish I could show you my country. Perhaps I will just take you out on the water now, for one short half-hour.'

He knew where a second boat was kept, and together they pushed it into the lake. As he rowed them towards the palace, he told Ralph about the festival, inventing details to disguise his ignorance. The wind began to strengthen, and then lightning flashed across the night sky, once, twice.

Ralph stared into the darkness. 'Was that the Rajah?' he asked.

'The Rajah? Where? No, sadly, the excitement was too much for the elderly gentleman and he died last night. It's a secret – I shouldn't have told you. We pretend he is alive until after the festival, to prevent unhappiness.'

'Row back. I can see the Rajah,' replied Ralph firmly.

Aziz followed the boy's instructions, and there, floating in the darkness, was a king in shining royal clothes, sitting on a golden chair . . . He had heard of the figure, a life-size representation of the Rajah's father, but he had never managed to see it before, although he frequently rowed on the lake. There was only one place where it could be seen, between the trees, and Ralph had directed him to it. Rapidly he rowed away from there, thinking that his companion was not so much a visitor as a guide.

Soon there was no need to row, as the freshening wind blew them in the right direction, and before long they found themselves at the water steps of the palace. The procession was descending the steps, with singers and dancers on either side. Down they stepped into the shallow water. Old Godbole saw

Aziz's boat, which was being blown towards the steps by the wind, and waved his arms – whether in anger or joy, Aziz never discovered. The storm worsened, sheets of rain fell from the sky, and the waves grew higher, as the priests prepared a silver dish full of tiny objects, representing the God, which would be thrown into the water. One of the priests, carrying the silver dish, entered the dark waters, while the singing around him reached its height. Then a great wave rose up, and English voices cried, 'Take care!'

The two boats had bumped into each other. The four outsiders tried to regain control, but the wind blew the boats towards the priest in the water, and they struck the dish he was holding. The shock made Stella fall into her husband's arms, which caused the boats to turn over. They all fell into the water, and came to the surface, struggling, to hear guns firing, drums beating, people shouting, and over it all an enormous clap of thunder.

The ceremony was at an end. Whatever had happened, had happened. The rain went on falling, the dish returned to Professor Godbole, the strangers picked themselves up, and the crowds of Hindus began to move slowly back to their homes.

The next day, friends again, yet aware that they would meet no more, Aziz and Fielding went out together for the last time, riding on horseback through the Mau jungle. The Rajah was now officially dead, and the visitors were departing the next day. From Fielding's professional point of view, the visit was a failure. He had hardly seen Godbole, who promised every day to show him round the King George Fifth School, but always made some excuse. Aziz finally explained that the school building was being used to store food, and Godbole did not like to admit to his former headmaster that no teaching at all was taking place. Fielding laughed at the waste of energy, but he did not travel as lightly as in the past. Education was a concern for him now, because his income and the comfort of his family depended on it.

But from the emotional point of view, the visit was a success. There was now no nonsense or bitterness, and he and Aziz went back laughingly to their old relationship, as if nothing had happened. They stopped for a moment to let a snake pass, and Aziz produced a letter that he wanted to send to Miss Quested. It was a charming letter, thanking his old enemy for her fine behaviour two years before.

Fielding was delighted, and said, 'I am glad you have seen her courage at last.'

'I want to do kindness all round, and forget about that miserable Marabar business for ever. I've been so stupidly quick to assume things, thinking you meant to get hold of my money – as bad a mistake as the cave itself.'

'Aziz, I wish you would talk to my wife. She has ideas – about the spirit – that I don't share. There's something she understands and I don't. Or talk to Ralph. He's a wise boy really. He's like her.'

'Tell him I have nothing to say to him, but he is indeed a wise boy and has always one Indian friend. I partly love him because he brought me back to you to say goodbye. Because this is goodbye, Cyril, although thinking about it will spoil our ride and make us very sad.'

Fielding too felt that this was their last chance to spend time together. All the stupid misunderstandings were gone, but socially they had no meeting-place. By marrying an Englishwoman, he had become part of British India, and was also becoming more fixed in his ideas as he grew older. He already felt some surprise at his own bravery in the past. Would he challenge his own people for the sake of just one Indian today? Aziz and he were proud of each other, but they had to part.

Aziz suddenly thought of something, and re-read his letter to Miss Quested. Hadn't he wanted to say something else to her? He took out his pen and added, 'From now on, I shall connect you with the name that is very holy in my mind, that is Mrs Moore.'

And all the way back to Mau, they argued about politics. Each had hardened his opinions since Chandrapore, and they greatly enjoyed their discussion. Fielding had 'no further use for politeness,' meaning that he saw no reason for the British to leave India because they were occasionally rude.

Aziz replied, 'Very well, and we have no use for you.'

Fielding said, 'Away from us, Indians lose all sense of purpose. Look at Godbole and the King George Fifth School! Look at you, forgetting about promotion and just writing poems.'

'They're very good poems.'

'Yes, and what do they say? "Free our women and India will be free." Try it, my friend. Free your own lady first, and see who'll wash Ahmed, Karim, and Jamila's faces. A nice situation!'

Aziz grew more excited. He cried, 'Get out, all you Turtons and Burtons. We wanted to know you ten years back – now it's too late. Get out, I say! Why do we have to suffer so much? We used to blame you, now we blame ourselves – we grow wiser. Until England is in difficulties we keep silent, but in the next European war – aha! Then is our time.'

They rode their horses past temples and shrines, through mud and water, between great trees with leaves like plates. And still they argued.

Aziz shouted, 'India shall be a nation! No foreigners of any sort! Hindu and Muslim and all shall be one! India! India! India!'

'One nation?' laughed Fielding. 'But you can never agree among yourselves!'

Furiously angry now, and not knowing what to do, Aziz made his horse dance this way and that. He cried, 'Down with the English, anyhow. That's certain. Get out, all of you, double quick, I say. We Indians may hate one another, but we hate you most. If I don't make you go, Ahmed will, Karim will! If it's fifty-five hundred years we shall get rid of you, yes, we shall drive every Englishman into the sea, and then' – he rode against him – 'and then,' he finished, half kissing him, 'you and I shall be friends.'

'Why can't we be friends now?' said the other, holding him close. 'It's what I want. It's what you want.'

But the horses didn't want it – they jumped apart; the earth didn't want it, sending up rocks through which riders must pass one by one; the temples, the lake, the palace, the birds, the guesthouse that came into view – they didn't want it, they said in their hundred voices, 'No, not yet,' and the sky said, 'No, not there.'

GLOSSARY

anti-British working against British interests

bazaar (in some Eastern countries) an area of town where there are many small shops

breasts the two round soft parts at the front of a woman's body

bungalow (in this story) a detached house

cabin a small room on a ship which you live or sleep in

career the series of jobs that a person has in a particular area of work

chap *(old-fashioned)* a man

compensation money that someone gives you because they have hurt you

courtyard an open space surrounded by the walls of a building

dignified calm, serious and deserving respect; **dignity** *(n)*

exile being sent to live in a country that is not your own

field-glasses binoculars, an instrument you look through and which makes distant objects seem nearer

fist a tightly closed hand with the fingers bent inwards

gentleman a polite, well-educated man who always behaves well

Good Heavens! an exclamation of surprise

groan to make a long deep sound because you are ill or unhappy

hag an ugly old woman

hallucination something seen or heard that is not really there

Hindu a person whose religion is Hinduism

holy connected with God or a particular religion

jungle an area of tropical forest where trees and plants grow very thickly

let (someone) off not to punish someone for something they have done wrong

level crossing a place where a road crosses a railway line

Lieutenant-Governor   (in this story) the chief British official in
  some Indian states
loose *(old-fashioned)*   immoral, ready to have sex with strangers
magistrate   an official who acts as a judge in the lowest lawcourt
Major   an officer of fairly high rank in the army
mango   a tropical fruit with smooth yellow or red skin, soft
  orange flesh and a large seed inside
Mogul Emperor   one of the Muslim race who ruled India from
  the 16th to the 19th century
morality   principles concerning right and wrong, or good and
  bad behaviour
mosque   a building in which Muslims worship
Muslim   a person whose religion is Islam
national anthem   the official song of a nation that is played or
  sung on special occasions
native   (in this story) a person who was born in India
plain *(n)*   a large area of flat land
polo   a game in which two teams of players riding on horses try
  to hit a ball into a goal using long wooden sticks
prosecution   the lawyers who try to prove in court that someone
  is guilty of a crime
pukka *(old-fashioned)*   appropriate for a particular social
  situation
purdah   the system in some Muslim societies in which women
  live in a separate part of the house so that men do not see
  them
race *(n)*   a group of people who share the same language, history,
  culture, etc.
Rajah   an Indian king or prince who ruled over a state in the past
rumour   a piece of information or a story which people talk
  about, but which may not be true
rupee   unit of money in India, Pakistan, and some other countries

sahib used in India in the past, for a European man, especially one of high social class or in an official position

sardines on toast tinned fish spread on toasted bread (a very traditional British meal in the past)

shrine a place where people come to worship because it is connected with a holy person or event

snub *(v & n)* to insult someone, especially by ignoring them when you meet

sob *(v & n)* to cry noisily

steamship a ship driven by steam

sting (of an insect) to make a very small hole in your skin so that you feel a sharp pain

strap a strip of leather that is used to carry something

stud a small metal object used in the past for fastening a collar on to a shirt

superior higher in rank, importance, or position

take sides to express support for one of the groups taking part in an argument

temple a building used for the worship of a god or gods

tropical coming from, or typical of, the tropics (the hottest part of the world)

Urdu a language used in Pakistan and India

veranda a platform with an open front and a roof, built on to the front of a house on the ground floor

ACTIVITIES

Before Reading

1 **Read the introduction on the first page of the book, and the back cover. What do you know now about *A Passage to India*? For each sentence, circle Y (Yes) or N (No).**

   1 The story is about Indians in Britain. Y / N
   2 Mrs Moore is Adela Quested's mother. Y / N
   3 Adela disapproves of the social attitudes of the British. Y / N
   4 Dr Aziz is an Indian headmaster. Y / N
   5 Adela may decide to marry Ronny Heaslop. Y / N
   6 Adela wants to meet Indian people. Y / N
   7 Mr Fielding suggests a visit to the Marabar Caves. Y / N

2 **Complete this passage about India's recent history by choosing one word from the pair of words given in brackets.**

   In the early 17th century the British set up permanent trading posts in India, each under the protection of a _____ (*native / foreign*) prince. By the 1850s, they had greatly expanded their _____ (*influence / economy*) in the area. In 1857, however, there was a rebellion by Indian soldiers who wanted to restore the _____ (*President / Mogul Emperor*) to power. Although this uprising was unsuccessful, the British took the opportunity to bring most of India under direct _____ (*parliament / rule*). Thousands of British _____ (*officers / officials*) spent their whole _____ (*careers / work*) in India, administering the country.
   A movement started by Mahatma Gandhi in 1920 finally led to India's _____ (*independence / statehood*) from Britain in 1947.

ACTIVITIES

While Reading

Read Chapters 1 to 4. Are these sentences true (T) or false (F)?
Rewrite the false sentences with the correct information.

1 Aziz approved of Mrs Moore's respect for the law.
2 Adela felt proud to be an Englishwoman in India.
3 Ronny was annoyed with Mr Turton for criticizing him.
4 Aziz was glad that he had invited the ladies to his home.
5 A car accident helped to bring Ronny and Adela together.
6 Fielding rejected Aziz's offer of friendship.

By the end of Chapter 4, what has changed for Adela, Ronny,
Fielding, Mrs Moore, and Aziz? Choose the phrase that best
describes the situation.

1 Adela understands *Ronny's character / a wife's duties* better.
2 Ronny is happy for Adela to *return to England / explore India*.
3 Fielding is *accepted by Aziz's friends / considered pukka by the
   Turtons*.
4 Mrs Moore has lost her *belief in God / desire to go home*.
5 Aziz is ready to *marry a second time / trust Fielding*.

Before you read Part Two (*Caves*), can you predict what happens
to these relationships?

1 Do Adela and Ronny break off their engagement?
2 Do Adela and Aziz become good friends?
3 Do Fielding and Aziz become lifelong friends?
4 Does Mrs Moore love her other children more than Ronny?

Read Chapters 5 to 8. Who said what to whom? Who or what were they talking about?

1 'This is the happiest moment of my life.'
2 'Never, never act the criminal.'
3 'People would never forgive you for that.'
4 'Oh, I'm being misunderstood, apologies.'
5 'I can't get rid of it.'
6 'Who cares what she thinks?'
7 'There are different ways of evil and I prefer mine to yours.'

Before you read Chapter 9 (*The trial*), can you guess what will happen? Circle Y (Yes) or N (No) for each of these ideas.

1 Fielding will prove Aziz's innocence. Y / N
2 Adela will withdraw her accusation. Y / N
3 The court will find Aziz guilty and send him to prison. Y / N

Read Chapters 9 to 13, and answer these questions.

1 How did the trial end, and why?
2 Why did Fielding look after Adela?
3 What happened to Mrs Moore?
4 Why did Aziz agree not to ask for compensation?
5 Why did Ronny break off his engagement?
6 What did Aziz suspect about Fielding?

Before you read Part Three (*Temple*), how do you think the story will end?

1 Will Adela or Fielding get married at the end of the story, and if so, who do you think they will marry?
2 Some of the characters meet two years later. Which ones?

ACTIVITIES

After Reading

1 Who's who in the story? Match the characters to their descriptions, and then to the sentences below.

Adela Quested	Ronny's half-brother
Ronny Heaslop	a doctor
Hamidullah	Ronny's mother
Mr McBryde	the local headmaster
Aziz	the City Magistrate
Ralph Moore	a friend of Ronny's
Mrs Moore	Aziz's aunt
Cyril Fielding	the city's chief official
Hamidullah Begum	a lawyer
Mr Turton	the Chief of Police

1 ... did not want society to punish criminals.
2 ... did not believe in God.
3 ... wanted to be as honest as possible.
4 ... always knew when someone was being unkind.
5 ... was worried about girls being unable to find husbands.
6 ... liked mysteries but disliked confusion.
7 ... thought that all Englishmen in India became exactly the same.
8 ... expected all English people to take the same attitude as him.
9 ... believed the reason the British were in India was to do justice and keep the peace.
10 ... thought that natives were more likely to commit crimes because of the effects of their climate.

2 **Here are the thoughts of seven characters before, during, or after the trip to the Marabar caves. Who is thinking, and at what point in the story? Choose the moment in time from the list below.**

a) on the train to Marabar   e) on the way back to Chandrapore
b) after arriving at Marabar   f) immediately after the arrest
c) on leaving the first cave   g) on hearing news of the arrest
d) just before entering the second cave

1 'I must remember, I'm not as young as I was. No wonder I get tired. But there was something I didn't like in there, something very frightening. It's still there, in my head. Why won't it go away? At least I can call on God for help . . . can I? . . . can I?'

2 'The thing is, love isn't everything. I have to accept that. I'm pretty sure he and I can be happy together, though. We'll have to work hard at it, of course. How do Indians manage this sort of thing, I wonder? My goodness, it's awfully hot! I hope there aren't many more of these wretched caves to see.'

3 'Look at Mohammed Latif! How much help is he, snoring away in his corner? I've so much to worry about – the tickets, the chairs, the food, the drinks, the elephant . . . it's enough to drive a fellow mad! Oh, I do wish the others hadn't missed the train!'

4 'What the devil's it all about? Some ridiculous complaint someone's made, I suppose – at the hospital, perhaps. Not a good way to end the confounded excursion. Well, it won't take long to sort out, and then we can all get some rest.'

5 'My God, I can't believe it – this is too awful for words! The poor girl looks terrible. How dare he! I'll just have to put my foot down and get her back to town as fast as possible. There's going to be serious trouble over this.'

6 'Dear me, that does seem an evil act. Hmm, yes, almost
certainly. But of course there is evil all around us, as there is
good all around us – that is the reality of the world we live in.
All we can do is ask God to be present. Yes, indeed. Nothing
more.'

7 'What an honour for me to assist such a respected friend of
the family on this most interesting excursion! To think that I
was actually riding on an elephant in the company of English
ladies! Now, I must make sure the servants serve the boiled
eggs correctly . . .'

3 **What actually happened in the cave at Marabar? A friend wrote to
E. M. Forster to ask this question. Read Forster's reply, and think
about the questions that follow.**

E. M. Forster: *'In the cave it is* either *a man,* or *the supernatural,*
or *an illusion. If I say, it becomes whatever the answer a different
book. And even if I know! My writing mind therefore is a blur
here – i.e. I will it to remain a blur, and to be uncertain, as I am of
many facts in daily life.'*

1 Which of the three ideas would you prefer as the explanation?
Explain why you think this. Would it make it a 'different book'?
2 Should Forster have given a clear indication of what happened?
Why do you think he wanted it to 'remain uncertain'? Are you,
like Forster, uncertain 'of many facts in daily life'?

4 **Do you agree or disagree with these ideas from the story?**

1 Happiness is just a dream.
2 It is good to travel light in life.
3 Being married once is enough for anyone.
4 Our purpose on earth is to love our neighbours.

5 **Fielding wrote a letter to Aziz, announcing his marriage (page 111). Choose words (one for each gap) to complete the letter.**

My dear Aziz,

Some news that will _____ you. I'm going to _____ someone you know. You _____ Mrs Moore, who you _____ so much? When I _____ to England recently, I _____ in touch with the _____ of Mrs Moore's second _____. I found Stella, her _____, to be a very _____ person. She is very _____ and is quick to _____ people's feelings and inner _____. To cut a long _____ short, we fell in _____. She has accepted my _____, despite the slight age _____ between us, and our _____ is in a fortnight's _____! I know you'll be _____ for me.

    Yours, Cyril

6 **Aziz did not read Fielding's letter, and Mahmoud Ali wrote the reply for Aziz (page 113). Choose words (one for each gap) to complete this letter.**

Dear Mr Fielding,

My friend Aziz has _____ me to write a _____ to your extremely unwelcome _____. He himself is too _____ to put pen to _____. It has been a _____ shock to hear you're _____ to marry Heaslop's sister. _____ your friendship for Aziz _____ nothing to you? He _____ and trusted you, but _____ repay him by insulting _____! By taking a wife _____ that particular family you _____ that you do not _____ about his friendship, and _____ no respect for his _____. Let me offer some _____: don't try to be _____ with us natives; just _____ to your own people _____ now on. Aziz hopes _____ to see you again.

    Sincerely, Mahmoud Ali

ABOUT THE AUTHOR

Edward Morgan Forster (1879–1970) was born in London. When he was only a year old, his father died, and Forster was brought up by his mother and his aunts. At the age of eight he inherited money from his great-aunt, which meant he never needed to earn a living. He studied classics at King's College, Cambridge, where he made some lifelong friends. After graduating, he went on the first of many trips to Europe with his mother, getting to know the Mediterranean culture he would later write about. When not travelling, he lived with his mother and worked on his writing. His first novel, *Where Angels Fear to Tread*, was published in 1905.

Soon after this, he became a private tutor in Latin to a young Indian called Syed Ross Masood. They became firm friends, and Masood gave Forster his first insights into India. As Forster wrote later, on the occasion of Masood's death: 'My own debt to him is incalculable. He woke me up out of my suburban and academic life, showed me new horizons and a new civilization, and helped me towards the understanding of a continent. Until I met him, India was a vague jumble of rajahs, sahibs, babus and elephants, and I was not interested in such a jumble; who could be? He made everything real and exciting as soon as he began to talk, and seventeen years later when I wrote *A Passage to India* I dedicated it to him out of gratitude as well as out of love, for it would never have been written without him.'

In the next few years Forster contributed to literary journals and published three more novels, *The Longest Journey* (1907), *A Room With a View* (1908), and *Howards End* (1910).

He made more Indian friends, Hindus as well as Muslims. Then in 1912 he set out to visit India for the first time. He kept what he called an Indian Diary, and sent many letters home to friends and family. These provided a useful record of his Indian experience, and formed the basis of his fifth novel, *A Passage to India*. He travelled widely in India, spending time in British communities as well as with Indians, but said that he 'almost always felt miserable in a Club, and almost always felt happy among Indians.' This is what he felt he had learnt from the trip: 'I had English friends in the civil service and I could pass from one camp to another with results that were interesting but painful. The English had been trained in a fine tradition of paternal government. Times were changing and they found it difficult to change. Some of them accepted the new situation with a good grace, most of them with a bad one, and the manners of their womenfolk could be ghastly. Looking back on that first visit of mine to India, I realize that mixed up with the pleasure and fun was much pain. The sense of racial tension, of incompatibility, never left me. It was not a tourist's outing, and the impression it left was deep.'

During World War I, Forster served in the Red Cross in Egypt. It was only after a second visit to India in the early 1920s that he managed to complete *A Passage to India*. Published in 1924, it became his most famous and widely translated work. It won the James Tait Memorial Prize and the Prix Femina Vie Heureuse, and it was made into a highly successful film.

At the age of 45 Forster stopped writing novels. He continued to write short stories and to lecture at Cambridge University, where he was a well-known and respected figure. He died in 1970 at the home of a friend and long-time companion. A sixth novel, *Maurice*, was published after his death.

OXFORD BOOKWORMS LIBRARY

Classics • Crime & Mystery • Factfiles • Fantasy & Horror
Human Interest • Playscripts • Thriller & Adventure
True Stories • World Stories

The OXFORD BOOKWORMS LIBRARY provides enjoyable reading in English, with a wide range of classic and modern fiction, non-fiction, and plays. It includes original and adapted texts in seven carefully graded language stages, which take learners from beginner to advanced level. An overview is given on the next pages.

All Stage 1 titles are available as audio recordings, as well as over eighty other titles from Starter to Stage 6. All Starters and many titles at Stages 1 to 4 are specially recommended for younger learners. Every Bookworm is illustrated, and Starters and Factfiles have full-colour illustrations.

The OXFORD BOOKWORMS LIBRARY also offers extensive support. Each book contains an introduction to the story, notes about the author, a glossary, and activities. Additional resources include tests and worksheets, and answers for these and for the activities in the books. There is advice on running a class library, using audio recordings, and the many ways of using Oxford Bookworms in reading programmes. Resource materials are available on the website <www.oup.com/bookworms>.

The *Oxford Bookworms Collection* is a series for advanced learners. It consists of volumes of short stories by well-known authors, both classic and modern. Texts are not abridged or adapted in any way, but carefully selected to be accessible to the advanced student.

You can find details and a full list of titles in the *Oxford Bookworms Library Catalogue* and *Oxford English Language Teaching Catalogues*, and on the website <www.oup.com/bookworms>.

THE OXFORD BOOKWORMS LIBRARY
GRADING AND SAMPLE EXTRACTS

STARTER • 250 HEADWORDS

present simple – present continuous – imperative –
can/cannot, must – *going to* (future) – simple gerunds …

Her phone is ringing – but where is it?

Sally gets out of bed and looks in her bag. No phone.
She looks under the bed. No phone. Then she looks behind
the door. There is her phone. Sally picks up her phone and
answers it. *Sally's Phone*

STAGE 1 • 400 HEADWORDS

… past simple – coordination with *and, but, or* –
subordination with *before, after, when, because, so* …

I knew him in Persia. He was a famous builder and I
worked with him there. For a time I was his friend, but
not for long. When he came to Paris, I came after him –
I wanted to watch him. He was a very clever, very dangerous
man. *The Phantom of the Opera*

STAGE 2 • 700 HEADWORDS

… present perfect – *will* (future) – *(don't) have to, must not, could* –
comparison of adjectives – simple *if* clauses – past continuous –
tag questions – *ask/tell* + infinitive …

While I was writing these words in my diary, I decided
what to do. I must try to escape. I shall try to get down the
wall outside. The window is high above the ground, but
I have to try. I shall take some of the gold with me – if I
escape, perhaps it will be helpful later. *Dracula*

STAGE 3 • 1000 HEADWORDS

... should, may – present perfect continuous – *used to* – past perfect –
causative – relative clauses – indirect statements ...

Of course, it was most important that no one should see
Colin, Mary, or Dickon entering the secret garden. So Colin
gave orders to the gardeners that they must all keep away
from that part of the garden in future. *The Secret Garden*

STAGE 4 • 1400 HEADWORDS

... past perfect continuous – passive (simple forms) –
would conditional clauses – indirect questions –
relatives with *where/when* – gerunds after prepositions/phrases ...

I was glad. Now Hyde could not show his face to the world
again. If he did, every honest man in London would be proud
to report him to the police. *Dr Jekyll and Mr Hyde*

STAGE 5 • 1800 HEADWORDS

... future continuous – future perfect –
passive (modals, continuous forms) –
would have conditional clauses – modals + perfect infinitive ...

If he had spoken Estella's name, I would have hit him. I was so
angry with him, and so depressed about my future, that I could
not eat the breakfast. Instead I went straight to the old house.
Great Expectations

STAGE 6 • 2500 HEADWORDS

... passive (infinitives, gerunds) – advanced modal meanings –
clauses of concession, condition

When I stepped up to the piano, I was confident. It was as if I
knew that the prodigy side of me really did exist. And when I
started to play, I was so caught up in how lovely I looked that
I didn't worry how I would sound. *The Joy Luck Club*

BOOKWORMS · HUMAN INTEREST · STAGE 6

The Joy Luck Club

AMY TAN

Retold by Clare West

There are so many things that a mother wishes to teach her daughter. How to lose your innocence but not your hope. How to keep hoping, when hope is your only joy. How to laugh for ever.

This is the story of four mothers and their daughters – Chinese-American women, the mothers born in China, and the daughters born in America. Through their eyes we see life in pre-Revolutionary China, and life in downtown San Francisco; women struggling to find a cultural identity that can include a past and a future half a world apart.

BOOKWORMS · CLASSICS · STAGE 6

Vanity Fair

WILLIAM THACKERAY

Retold by Diane Mowat

When Becky Sharp and Amelia Sedley leave school, their feet are set on very different paths. Kind, foolish Amelia returns to her comfortable home and wealthy family, to await a suitable marriage, while Becky must look out for herself, earning her own living in a hard world. But Becky is neither kind nor foolish, and with her quick brain and keen eye for a chance, her fortunes soon rise, while Amelia's fall.

Greed, ambition, loyalty, betrayal, folly, wisdom . . . Thackeray's famous novel gives us a witty and satirical picture of English society during the Napoleonic wars.